PRAISE FOR
THE FRUGAL EDITOR

Carolyn Howard-Johnson has done it again! Whether you're writing your first book or tenth, *The Frugal Editor* is a must-read.
~ Tim Bete, director, Erma Bombeck Writers' Workshop (humorwriters.org/)

Carolyn Howard-Johnson has created a practical guide to editing your work. You'll want to keep it handy and refer to it every time you finish a piece of work whether it is a query letter, a simple pitch, or a novel. Use her system step-by-step and you will very likely see your work change from an attractive lump of coal to a polished diamond editors won't be able to refuse.
~ Magdalena Ball, editor and owner of CompulsiveReader.com

In this invaluable (and yes, accessible and engaging, too!) resource, Carolyn Howard-Johnson masterfully elevates an oft-misunderstood practice into the critical component of writing that it is. Don't turn in anything until you turn to this book.
~ Peter Bowerman, author of *The Well-Fed Writer* series (wellfedwriter.com)

Using the basic computer and editing tricks from *The Frugal Editor*, authors can prevent headaches and save themselves time—and even money—during the editing process. It's well worth your effort to learn them.
~ Barbara McNichol, Barbara Editorial (wordtrippers.com/)

Howard-Johnson hits the nail on the head with *The Frugal Editor*. She points out the gremlins and simplifies the eradication process. What more could a writer/editor/publisher ask for?
~ Peggi Ridgway, author of *Successful Web site Marketing* and other business books

The Frugal Editor: Do-it-yourself editing secrets for authors: From your query letter to final manuscript to the marketing of your new bestseller will become a well-used reference for writers around the world.
~ Cheryl Wright, editor of Writer2Writer.com

Good editing is like honest business accounting: If you don't have it, you end up with a mess. *The Frugal Editor* is a must for the novice writer who needs to make that ideal first impression and the writer with a tenth book hitting the shelves who has become complacent about his or her brilliant prose.
~ Kristin Johnson, author and writing consultant

Nothing demonstrates professionalism like a well-edited submission. Follow Carolyn Howard-Johnson's clear, step-by-step self-editing approach for putting your best book forward and you'll submit like a pro.
~ Gregory A. Kompes, conference coordinator of The Las Vegas Writer's Conference

Careers that are not fed die as readily as any living organism given no sustenance.

The
Frugal Editor
Second Edition

Do-it-yourself editing secrets for authors:
From your query letter to final manuscript
to the marketing of your new bestseller

By Carolyn Howard-Johnson

HowToDoItFrugally Publishing
Los Angeles
Originally Published by Red Engine Press
Key West

ISBN-13: 978-1505712117
ISBN-10: 1505712114
BISAC: BUS011000, BUS052000
ASIN: E-book, B0011EK6VC
1. English language—Rhetoric 2. Creative writing 3. Writing—Authorship
Cover by Chaz DeSimone of DesimoneDesign.com
Three Dimensional Cover Image by Gene Cartwright of iFOGO.com/3D/. AKA Amazon List Network
Author Photograph by Uriah Carr
Logo by Lloyd King
Paperback printed in the United States of America

Quantity discounts are available on bulk purchases of this book for educational institutions, social organizations, or nonprofits. For information, please contact HoJoNews@aol.com

This book is available at a discount when purchased in quantity to use as premiums, sales promotions, in corporate training programs, or by schools or social organizations for educational purposes. For information, please contact HowToDoItFrugally Publishing at HoJoNews@aol.com.

First edition published by Red Engine Press, 2007

This book is an updated edition of *The Frugal Editor: Put your best book forward to avoid humiliation and ensure success* (2007). It is the second in the HowToDoItFrugally series of books for writers, not to be confused with another HowToDoItFrugally series for retailers. *The Frugal Editor* has a new subtitle to accommodate the expanded subject matter. This new edition comes to you with the gentle reminder that in the Internet world, retailers (and most anyone else in the business community) must also be editors. They are bloggers, advertising copywriters, sign makers, and publicists because they often write the media releases for their own marketing efforts. That they must multi task is nothing new, but in this quickly changing world, everyone is more responsible than ever for the success of his or her own project—from beginning to end, and that often includes the editing.

The cover of this book, designed by Chaz DeSimone, uses American Typewriter font from International Typeface Corporation to suggest a writer's typewritten manuscript, and ITC's Century Condensed to emulate the typeset composition of a printed book. The interior of this book is set in Times New Roman, a highly legible font traditionally used for books and newspapers.

Careers that are not fed die as readily as any living organism given no sustenance.

IN MEMORY OF

Trudy McMurrin, 1944-2009, university press director and editor extraordinaire from whom I learned so much. She edited the first edition of this book.

Careers that are not fed die as readily as any living organism given no sustenance.

The
Frugal Editor
Second Edition

Do-it-yourself editing secrets for authors: From your query letter to final manuscript to the marketing of your new bestseller

By Carolyn Howard-Johnson

HowToDoItFrugally Publishing
Los Angeles

WHY THIS BOOK IS PART OF THE HOWTODOITFRUGALLY SERIES

1. I know that though I give authors guidelines for hiring the editor best suited to a specific title, many will not hire one because they, too, are frugal, or because they are so confident of their own skills they deem such a service unnecessary (a danger sign, by the way).

2. I know that the more an author knows about editing, the better partner she or he will be for the editor she hires or the one assigned to her by her publisher, and the more secure she or he will be about accepting or rejecting suggested edits.

3. I know some authors are unable to discern the difference between an editor and a typo hunter and will hire underqualified editors. This book prepares authors to recognize this disaster if it should occur. If you come to this realization, you might need to start over with another, more capable editor. Or you might be able to step in and fix what your editor missed.

4. I know that the cleaner the copy an author hands an editor, the more accurate the editor can be. It might also cost the author less for editors who charge by the hour.

Careers that are not fed die as readily as any living organism given no sustenance.

CONTENTS

WHY THIS BOOK IS PART OF THE HOWTODOITFRUGALLY SERIES   X

ACKNOWLEDGEMENTS   XV

BEFORE WE GET STARTED Gremlins, Horses, Writers and You   xix
   WHY YOU—YES, YOU WHO ACED ENGLISH—NEED THIS BOOK
   LEADING A HORSE TO WATER AND OTHER ALL-WET IDEAS
    ABOUT EDITING
   HAVE YOU EVER RUN ACROSS A GREMLIN?

SECTION ONE
THE PRELIMINARIES   27

ONE: MISUNDERSTANDING EDITING   29

TWO: ORGANIZING ONLY FEELS LIKE PROCRASTINATION   33
   YOUR DESKTOPS   33

THREE: BEST BOOK FORWARD: GREAT EDITING *IS* GREAT BRANDING 41

SECTION TWO
THE HANDIWORK OF PUBLISHING   43

FOUR: MANUSCRIPTS: LETTING THE HARDCOPIES FLY   45

FIVE: DANGEROUS CORNERS AHEAD: COVERS AND QUERIES   49

SIX: LET'S MAKE EVERYONE AGREE   55

SEVEN: CUT-AND-PASTE ERRORS: THE WAY TO A GREMLIN'S HEART 59

EIGHT: PEEKING INTO THE MINDS AND INBOXES OF AGENTS   61

SECTION THREE

LET YOUR COMPUTER DO WHAT IT DOES BEST 71

NINE: USE WORD'S TOOLS; DON'T TRUST THEM 73
CONSIDER THE SOURCE: TRACKING 75
WORD'S UNDISCERNING, BUT THOROUGH EDITING TOOL 78
EXTRA SPACES ARE LIKE FLUFF BALLS UNDER THE BED 82
YOUR UNTRUSTWORTHY SPELLING AND GRAMMAR CHECK 85
YOUR CUSTOM DICTIONARY: MAKING IT PERSONAL 87
READABILITY STATS AND WORD COUNTS KEEP YOU ON YOUR TOES 92
YOUR OWN STYLE GUIDE 93
USING SHORTCUTS FOR THE STUFF WRITERS NEED 98

SECTION FOUR

EDITING FOR STRONGER WRITING 105

TEN: HUNTING DOWN YOUR DREADED ADVERBS 107
THE OBVIOUS *LY* ADVERBS 107
IS THIS ADVERB RELATED TO *Y'KNOW?* 109
DOES THIS ADVERB MAKE YOUR VERBS LOOK SILLY? 112
EDITING YOUR ADVERBS IS LIKE MINING METAPHOR GOLD 114

ELEVEN: DEATH TO GERUNDS, PARTICIPLES, AND OTHER UGLY *INGS* 117
DANGLING PARTICIPLES OFTEN COME WITH TATTLETALE *INGS* 118
GERUNDS KEEP YOU FROM LAUGHING ALL THE WAY TO THE BANK 120
A PARTICIPLE *ING* IS NOT A GERUND'S TWIN 121
WAS-*ING* AND WERE-*ING* 122

TWELVE: WIPE OUT INEFFECTIVE PASSIVES 125

THIRTEEN: GETTING RID OF DIALOGUE MIGRAINES 131
AMATEUR DIALOGUE TAGS CAN BE BIG HEADACHES 133
DIALOGUE PUNCTUATION HEADACHES 136

SECTION FIVE

CANDY AND VEGGIES FOUND IN THE MEDIA 141

**FOURTEEN: VIRUSES AREN'T THE ONLY COMMUNICABLE DISEASE
CONTRACTED FROM THE NET**   143
   GETTING CUTE WITH CAPS   144
   EFFUSIVE ITALICS   146
   QUOTATION MARKS FOR THE TOO-DUMB READER?   148
   QUESTION MARKS AND EXCLAMATION POINTS RUNNING AMOK 152
   ELLIPSIS DOTS GONE WILD   152
   AMPERSANDS: PRETTY IS AS PRETTY DOES   155
   SIMPLIFY POSSESSIVES SO GREMLINS CAN'T MESS WITH YOU 156
   OTHER FRIGHTENING APOSTROPHES   160
   YOU'RE A WRITER: YOU GET TO MAKE UP WORDS   164
   MYRIAD USES FOR HYPHENS   169
   WHAT ABOUT THOSE DOUBLE ADJECTIVES?   174
   BLAMING THE NET, THE MEDIA, AND EVEN LINGUISTICS   176
   WORDINESS, CLICHÉS, AND POLITICALLY CORRECT   185
   THE DREADED CLAUSE INTRODUCERS   189

SECTION SIX
FINAL HOUSECLEANING   193

FIFTEEN: YOU'RE B-A-A-A-CK: TWO FINAL, MANUAL EDITS   195
   NEXT-TO-LAST MANUAL EDIT FOR PROFESSIONAL CONSUMPTION 195
   YOUR FINAL, FINAL EDIT   200
   ARE YOU CONVINCED YOU STILL DON'T NEED AN EDITOR? 201

SIXTEEN: GALLEY EDITS: BELIEVING IN GREMLINS   209
   TRICKS TO FOIL THE GALLEY GREMLINS   210

SEVENTEEN: GOING IT ON YOUR OWN   219
   YOUR PUBLISHING EDUCATION WEB-STYLE   222

EIGHTEEN: PUTTING YOUR WORK OUT INTO THE WORLD   225
WHEN MAIL IS YOUR FIRST FOOT IN THE DOOR   227
WHEN E-MAIL IS PREFERRED   229

APPENDICES   233

APPENDIX ONE: EDITING AT A GLANCE   235

APPENDIX TWO: RECOMMENDED READING AND RESOURCES   237
EDITING   237
EDITORS   238
GRAMMAR AND STYLE   238
WRITING CRAFT   240
CUSTOM DICTIONARIES   241
PUBLISHING, PROMOTION, AND MARKETING   241
BOOK PROPOSALS   242
TYPESETTING AND/OR FORMATTING   242
HAVING FUN   243
DIRECTORIES: MARKETPLACES FOR YOUR WORK   243

APPENDIX THREE: "MY" GENEROUS LITERARY AGENTS   245

APPENDIX FOUR: SAMPLE COVER LETTERS   247
SAMPLE LETTER FOR A MEDIA KIT   248
SAMPLE LETTER FOR SUBMISSIONS TO JOURNALS, CONTESTS   249

APPENDIX FIVE: SAMPLE QUERY LETTERS   251
SAMPLE QUERY LETTER FOR FILM CONSIDERATION—FICTION   251
SAMPLE QUERY LETTER FOR A PUBLISHER—NONFICTION   253
SAMPLE QUERY LETTER FOR AN AGENT—FICTION   254

APPENDIX SIX: FORMATTING FOR KINDLE MADE EASY   257

APPENDIX SEVEN: OTHER FRUGAL RESOURCES FOR WRITERS   263

ABOUT THE AUTHOR   265

INDEX   273

ACKNOWLEDGEMENTS

Inspiration comes from unexpected places. Years ago when I was interviewing for an instructor's position at UCLA Extension Writers' Program, I mentioned that unsuspecting authors needed information on book promotion that I'd learned from the School of Hard Knocks. Linda Venis, the director of the Writers' and Literature Programs, loved the idea and thought that a course based on this idea was a good idea. So, thank you, Linda. Thank you, UCLA.

But horrors. That interview was, perhaps, in February or March. I now had a class to teach that fall quarter and I could see how having a book that covered everything on public relations and marketing for books to practical ideas for doing so was needed. That wasn't enough time to query an agent, much less get a book published and released. Enter Kristie Leigh Maguire, an author I knew from the Web. She had been a publisher in one of her former lives, was starting a new company, and said she could get *The Frugal Book Promoter* out in plenty of time for my class. Thank you, Kristie. Thank you, Star Publish.

That brings me to this book. Joyce Faulkner, publisher at Red Engine Press, asked me to write a couple of sections for a book on editing she was publishing. I thought if I was going to do that, I should also propose a class on that subject to UCLA. They accepted. It turned out I needed a text for that class as well. Thank you, Joyce. Thank you, UCLA (again). Thanks to the many hundreds of authors who wrote to tell me how much they appreciate what *The Frugal Editor* did for them. Without them, there might have been no second edition of this book.

Thanks go to all you emerging and experienced authors whose typos and booboos gave me so many more ideas that a mere chapter for Joyce's original concept would not cover them all. And to my editing helpers, Trudy McMurrin, Lance Johnson, author of *What Foreigners Need To Know About America From A To Z* published by Oriental Press in China and A To Z Publishing in English in the US.

Thanks to two writers, supporters, and friends who have been with me since before my first book was published, JayCe Crawford and Leora Krygier. Thanks to Marilyn Ross, Magdalena Ball, Tim Bete, Peter Bowerman, Kathe Gogolewski, Peggi Ridgway, Kristin Johnson, Dr. Bob Rich, Chaz DeSimone, and Gene Cartwright—all inspirations and experts known for helping authors in myriad ways.

I can't forget the literary agents quoted in this book, agents who were generous enough to help me help you avoid the pitfalls so many writers fall into when composing their query letters.

I'd also like to thank the malicious gremlins, the *raisons d'être* for this book. They're the ones who put a damper on the publication of my first book, a novel called *This Is the Place*, and have continued to harass me to one degree or another ever since. Experience is the best teacher and now, I hope, my gremlin-slaying experiences will inform and inspire you.

I hope the best lesson gleaned from this journey is that no author is an island. This book is not meant to encourage you to be one, but on those occasions when you must be, it will be a good aid and companion. On those occasions when you have great editing help, you *will* feel more secure about accepting or rejecting edits and about partnering with that editor.

Careers that are not fed die as readily as any living organism given no sustenance.

BEFORE WE GET STARTED
Gremlins, Horses, Writers and You

WHY YOU—YES, YOU WHO ACED ENGLISH—NEED THIS BOOK

As I was putting the last touches on this book, *Poets & Writers* published Peter Selfin's "Confessions of a Cranky Lit-Mag Editor." It was a mini rant on how authors annoy editors with unseen errors. He tells of one author who informs him in her cover letter that she has published three stories in *The New Yorker* and then "blunders into her essay with the dangling modifier 'Growing up, there were two types of food in my family.'" He says it "reads like very sloppy editing," and he goes on to reject the piece.

By the way, one of my readers with a master's degree could not identify the error here. If you can't, you will be able to do so by the time you've finished Chapter Eleven in this book where I talk about dangling participles.

The lesson for all of us is that attention to detail and craft counts, and that even experienced writers can flub an opportunity if they don't pay attention to that last great step toward publishing, a good edit. Any author who refreshes her understanding of participles by reading this book would not dangle hers. At least not that conspicuously.

Perfection is not possible. Even Editor Selfin admits he overlooks a mistake or two if the writer's voice captures his interest. With better editing you can guard against humiliation and in the process increase your chances for publication.

LEADING A HORSE TO WATER AND OTHER ALL-WET IDEAS ABOUT EDITING

In my first how-to book, *The Frugal Book Promoter*, I talk about branding. When I wrote it, I felt a need to convince authors that sales, marketing, and promotion are not dirty words, that we are participating in these disciplines every day when we brush our teeth and choose the proper clothing for whatever occasions loom on that day's calendar.

I don't need to convince most authors to be cautious about grammar errors and typos. So many writers are so uptight about a typo creeping into their copy that their fear contributes to nightmares or at least to writer's block. Thus, *The Frugal Editor: Do-it-yourself editing secrets for authors: From your query letter to final manuscript to the marketing of your new bestseller* is an easy sell.

Where my job becomes difficult is in convincing writers that they need an editor—a real editor, an editor with credentials—before they begin to submit. Because I am also frugal, I recognize that my tendency to avoid spending money for something that will probably be done by someone else (or that I'm just as good at) might well exist in other writers.

I know that many writers will nod their heads and then attempt the publishing process without an editor, even though they might have had the best intentions when they were agreeing with me. I am also aware (because I hang out with writers of all kinds) that authors fear the sharp pencil point of an editor. They are usually new writers who are convinced that an editor will tinker with their voice, try to make their work into something other than what it is, or will change it beyond recognition. I want to assure these writers that a good editor won't do that. A good editor helps a writer find her voice, remain true to it, and still move the manuscript from a rough rock to a polished gemstone.

> **Note:** Many writers mistake some things—like wordiness and clichés—for "voice." A good editor can help a writer clean up her copy without losing its distinguishing qualities. She might even help the author find a more resonant voice without relying on questionable structure and grammar.

It is no fun to encounter unexpected flaws in your book. However, mistakes in your query letters, cover letters, and book proposals can be more deadly than those in your manuscript. Choices that go against publishing industry traditions for these documents can doom your entire book to failure. You and the quality of your book idea will be judged on these first contacts with agents, publishers, editors, and producers as surely as you would be judged at a board meeting if you left rats' nests in your hair that morning. It's these seemingly inconsequential documents that you must generally edit on your own.

So, in this book, I approach the editing process of every document as if it were a manuscript. It is easier to edit the much shorter introductions (query letters, cover letters, media kits, and proposals) that are sent to the people who have the power to accept or reject your work, but the processes used are approximately the same. It is only a matter of degree between a full manuscript and your one-page query letter. So adapt the guidelines I give you accordingly. You, and only you, know where your strengths and weaknesses lie. You will know where to abbreviate or eliminate steps for these shorties, and for more intricate efforts (say, an academic thesis). You can expand on the processes I've suggested and double check with the style guides your university almost certainly has available to help you with that endeavor. Preferences *do* differ from one school to the other.

You probably already know that gremlins—very clever guys bent on chaos—are at work during the entire publishing process. You fight them with every ounce of writing craft and publishing knowledge that exists in your body. If, however, a typo or grammar error slips through the careful net you cast for them, please don't lose any sleep. It will happen to every writer somewhere along her career path. Instead, be patient with yourself.

And while you're at it, if you see an error in someone else's work, give the writer (and the publisher) the benefit of the doubt. It's all about Karma. We're all fighting the same gremlins here.

Many mistakenly use the word *editing* synonymously with finding typos. I worry that *The Frugal Editor* might contribute to that notion because it does not address essential elements of the writing craft like character development, setting, or structure. Those are topics of their own. Reworking these aspects of writing constitutes *revision*, not editing. Many complete books cover each of these writing skills thoroughly. For me to attempt to stipulate everything a polished manuscript needs would be impossible in one book. To cover revision topics briefly and then abandon the writer to struggle with incomplete understanding would not be in her or his best interest. Because I can't assume that all authors revise before they move into editing, I urge you to consider these writing fundamentals. Experienced writers can approach revision with the expectation that they might need to fine-tune only one or two elements of their books, but even minor learning curves are journeys worth taking. One of my favorite books for this final work on a manuscript of fiction is *Wired for Story* (bit.ly/WiredStory) by Lisa Cron (Ten Speed Press). An editor like Barbara McNichol (barbaramcnichol.com) can help an author of nonfiction fill out, fill in, and organize.

Though I include some basic grammar guidelines in this book, they are not meant to be complete. There are thousands of books on grammar and whole graduate programs on grammar and structure. I chose just a few of the mistakes that many experienced writers (and editors) miss. I threw in a few of the ones that most writers understand but inadvertently make because when a writer does let them creep into her work, they are more noxious to my editing sensibility than the average error. I expect that when I mention some you already know, it will remind you not to backslide. It might even prompt you to check your references for more information on those subjects. I also mention a few that the average person is rarely tested by, but that writers run into all the time. *Entitled* is an example of one of these. I mention it in Chapter Five along with several other author blunders that annoy agents and acquisition editors.

I want you to learn from this book just as I learned from writing it, but I'd also like you to enjoy the editing challenge, the process itself. Pretend the task before you is a puzzle. It's work. It's *detailed* work. Still, it can be a lot of fun.

HAVE YOU EVER RUN ACROSS A GREMLIN?

If a gremlin were only the guy with purple warts on his head in the Lamisil ad, I wouldn't worry about him. You know, the one who causes toenails to yellow, the fellow you try to eradicate at the risk of executing your liver. According to the commercials, that gremlin is easy to avoid. Simply ask your doctor for Lamisil.

If you imagine the gremlin as the ogre who hid under your bed when you were a kid and cleverly disappeared when your parents peeked under to search for him, well, he hasn't reappeared in decades. If you imagine him as the chap who showed up in fairy tales so you wouldn't get bored, you might welcome him as inspiration for a short story.

But no. He is the lowdown creep who makes passive construction (See Chapter Twelve) reappear in your manuscript after you've edited it over and over again. He has enough relatives to plague every writer in existence. You can't see these gremlins, but you'll know they have been at work when your book appears in print. Telltale signs will crop up in typos, grammar errors, widows, orphans, and other ugly formatting problems. So I worry about them a lot. You should, too.

I can't tell you how to eliminate these gremlins. After all, there are homicide laws. I *can* tell you how to make their job harder. You must recognize they exist, purge any inclination you might have toward assassination, and let someone else bring them to justice. For as real as these gremlins are—regardless of how often we're told they're "only imaginary"—there is a myth that's passed on to us as truth. That's the story authors believe about editors and publishers.

We writers believe these stories because it's convenient to think that magical personages hired by publishers make books come off the press in immaculate form. Perfect. Pristine. That can happen, but I've come upon an occasional typo in books that are published by revered names in our industry. A few exist in my own books—more in some than in others. Some showed up before I knew I had to take charge of my own books' destinies. Some showed up after I knew that, but didn't know much about my part in editing. Some occasionally turn up secretly when I have the nerve to eliminate one of his comrades. You can trust my hard-won experience when I tell you it behooves an author to do the very best she can—on her own—to eradicate the gremlins' work. If these troublemakers get one up on Random House and Farrar, Straus & Giroux, other publishers and authors are easy touches.

So, how to do what seems to elude the best and brightest of word warriors? That's what I'm here for— to pass along antidotes for what I see most frequently in the critique groups I facilitate and the classes I teach.

Some of this information will seem basic, but you need to know the gremlin's secret. His motto is, "When authors and editors are looking for the big stuff,

I'll diddle with the puny mistakes they're not likely to see." Gremlins are devious. They are not above going after more humiliating errors that anyone can spot, like using apostrophes in plurals. (Learn more about frightening apostrophes in Chapter Fourteen.) They know your weak moments, your tired moments.

The Frugal Editor is also designed for user-friendly research and to make the editing process easier and more thorough. You'll find information that you will refer to time and again in the boxes titled "Sidebar." I also include an Index. (Your teachers weren't exaggerating when they lauded the usefulness of indexes.)

You'll also learn both manual and computer techniques for digging errors out of your copy and keeping them out.

The most important part of the editing process is getting over the idea that someone else will do this for you or that it doesn't matter. It matters big. When you submit queries to agents. When you submit proposals to publishers. When your publisher submits a galley for you to examine and authorize. So bear with me. Make the guidelines in this book part of your work habits. You'll need several tricks up your sleeve to keep all the gremlins at bay.

SECTION ONE

THE PRELIMINARIES

CHAPTER ONE
MISUNDERSTANDING EDITING

One of the big problems with editing is that people misunderstand the word. Or they assign several meanings to it so that no one appears to fully understand what others are talking about. Further, innovations in the publishing industry, market upheavals, and shifting responsibilities have changed the definitions of editing, proofreading, galleys, and other publishing terms in the past decades. Here is a mini-glossary so that as you and I work together, we'll be using a similar dictionary.

- **Revision**—Revision is a lot more than editing. It is reworking your piece before you start the editing process, though you may perform some editing functions in the process. (Don't we all edit a little every time we sit down at a keyboard or pick up a pen?) It applies more to manuscripts than to short presentations like query and cover letters. It is the work you do between the first draft and the second, tenth, or twentieth.

- **Editing**—This is what fine publishing houses used to do for all of their authors. They helped with the revision process and everything else until your manuscript was a butterfly in repose. No more. Leora Krygier, who has published traditionally with several fine small presses says, "Publishers do not want to edit anymore—they want to print a ninety-nine percent finished product directly from the author." It's a cost-cutting thing. Many publishers can't afford to give your book the attention they once did. If you want to be sure your precious book gets a full edit, hire an editor. I give you tips on how to do this as successfully as possible in Chapter Fifteen.

- **Line Editing**—This is what you'll get—if anything—from most publishers today whether they are on your publisher's staff or are independent contractors. The quality may be good . . . or not. A line editor will catch style problems, most grammar errors, and your typo and spelling errors. They probably won't do anything with organization, structure, or writing technique. The cleaner the copy you submit, the more easily he or she can spot the tricky details.

- **Proofreading**—Proofreaders are typo hunters. Some might be insulted if you call them that, but that's what they are hired for—generally at low wages. Many "editors" you hire yourself (often without being careful about getting recommendations or about researching credentials) are capable of doing little more than typo hunting. Just the basics, Ma'am. Punctuation, spelling, typos, a modicum of grammar. The ones employed by publishers rather than by you might not be authorized to edit or rewrite so they simply suffer in silence when they run across your dangling participles. Ditto when your dialogue tags (those indicators that let a reader know who is speaking) need some work or when your structure is out of whack.

> **Note**: We love the English teachers in our lives but they are not editors. Most know nothing about the publishing world. They probably won't be able to help with many aspects of publishing and they may even apply grammar "rules" to parts of our manuscripts where they aren't appropriate. Stay tuned for more on why dialogue and other parts of our creative work may be—in fact sometimes *should* be—ungrammatical.

This book will help you with all of these processes—even a few techniques that would normally be tackled during revision, like writing dialogue tags. Clearly, you will be practicing your editing skills from the first time you put fingers-to-keyboard—both the skills you already have and the ones you learn from this book, but your final edit will go much more smoothly if you first *revise* your manuscript using all your skills no matter how or when you acquired them.

CHAPTER TWO
ORGANIZING ONLY FEELS
LIKE PROCRASTINATION

Setting up your surroundings for the editing process is so much fun it might feel as if you're procrastinating. Relish the experience. Clear your desk of piles of stuff so tall you can't see over them, but don't be tempted to take on the tasks you find buried in them; they waited this long, they can wait longer. Put the papers, notebooks, and clippings aside or file them and enjoy feeling naughty. When your environment is about as tidy as it will ever get, you're ready to get your editing tools in shape.

YOUR DESKTOPS

Your real old-fashioned desk environment

Put your most important real-life reference books on your desk near your computer even if you prefer to use online resources. You should be able to reach them without moving your fanny from your chair. Here are some essentials I recommend. Some can't be accessed online without paying for them, so why not have a hardcopy readily available.

- *The Chicago Manual of Style* (bit.ly/ChiStBk) is your preferred reference when you're writing a book.
- *Associated Press* Stylebook (bit.ly/AssocPressStyle) is your preferred reference for making style choices for writing for most of the new media, newspapers, and magazines. Notice that most sources list *stylebook* as a single word but *style guide* as two.
- Your favorite thesaurus.
- A good dictionary. Microsoft Word's language functions are not a substitute.
- Any special vocabulary dictionaries your project requires. These include dictionaries for dialect, jargon, scientific terms, tech terms, or discipline-specific stylebooks.
- *The Complete Rhyming Dictionary* (bit.ly/ComRhyme) by Clement Wood. Many writers who are not poets occasionally find alliteration, assonance, and rhyme useful tools for leads, headlines, titles, and copywriting—if not in their creative writing, in their marketing.
- *The Describer's Dictionary* (bit.ly/Describers) by David Grambs. Nonfiction writers might find this book as useful as fiction writers and poets do.

> **Note**: You might be surprised that I do not list *Elements of Style* (bit.ly/ElementsStyle) by Strunk, White, and Angell among my favorites. *Strunk* is a *stylebook* that gets mistaken for a book of grammar rules. It often confuses writers who aren't trained editors. We'll

talk about style choices vs. grammar rules later. If you have a copy of *Strunk* already, check the copyright date. *Strunk* has been through many editions over the years and the old ones might lead you astray big time.

Get your computer ready to edit

If you don't work with Word's Spelling and Grammar Checker all the time, set it up. (Find instructions for using your checker in the "Your Flawed Friend" information box in this chapter.

Stow the online references you need for this project somewhere in your computer where they can be easily accessed. If you need a style guide for writing technical material, Google or go to inews.berkeley.edu/guide/style#b280. For computer terms, check pc.net/glossary/.

Avoid computer confusion

Many writers already have systems in place to avoid computer confusion. Others use their computers almost like a word processor or typewriter. Those whose skills don't go much beyond typing and e-mail and a little Facebook fun might need to be reminded how to avoid accessing an old manuscript copy from your computer's memory during the editing process. To do that you:

- **Save** your rough draft or the revised copy of your manuscript with the title and a code to indicate it is your original, something like "ThisLandDividedOrig010114." Because I still don't quite trust computers (or electricity), I also run a hardcopy and file it. I also backup using Microsoft's Onedrive and e-mail important stuff to my daughter for safekeeping on her Mac.

- Once you've saved your original, click on **Save As** to make a new file. Some tech gurus and editors prefer using file names with just the title and date. Dr. Bob Rich says, "A good system of file nomenclature is 'title yymmdd,' e.g., 'frugaleditor01032014.docx.'"
- Label every page in your manuscript with the name of the current file of your book by using the header/footer function in your Word program. That way, no matter where you work within the manuscript—whether online or offline—you will be less likely to work with an outdated file. You'll also find that confirming (and soothing) information in the top bar of your screen near the Word icon. The bar will be blue unless you've customized your screen colors.

Set up a basic page layout for your manuscript. Here are suggestions based on what most agents and publishers ask for. By doing so, you'll avoid making drastic changes to basic layout later. Here's how:

- Set your Word program's **Page Layout** for *manuscripts*. Word provides a lot of automated themes and layouts. Avoid them. Keep it simple.
- You'll probably be OK with margins one inch all around.
- Set for double space.
- Put page numbers in the **Header** on the right (if you install them on the left, they will not

be visible when the pages are paperclipped). Include your full name in the header unless the manuscript is being submitted for a contest. (Contest guidelines will let you know.)

- This is *not* the time to save paper by printing on both sides.
- Don't flirt with fancy typefaces for your titles. Don't you dare play with sans serif typeface like Arial (fonts with no little hats or feet on the tops and bottoms of each letter). In my opinion, sans serif is elegant. Still, research tells us that it is more difficult to read, most editors will be unimpressed by your effort, and some will be downright annoyed. I submitted my first poetry book manuscript to an untold number of contests (and sometimes paid fees) before I discovered that many contest readers junk entries without reading them as soon as they run across the poems' titles formatted in anything sans serif. That affectation apparently shouts, "Novice! No need to continue reading!" They probably miss some poems of pure genius but who am I (or you) to argue with a gatekeeper?

> **Note**: Reformat only if your gatekeeper asks for something else and be sure to save the one you have and reformat in a new document with a new file name.

To keep the editing process from becoming daunting, tackle the manuscript with one kind of edit at a time. Start with a relatively easy project or something creative to get you in the mood for the big job you are about to undertake. I begin with a search for adverbs. You'll find more on adverb search and seizure in Chapter Ten, "Hunting Down Your Dreaded Adverbs."

Schedule enough time to do an individual editing project at one sitting. Doing bits of a job here and there plays into the hands of gremlins. You'll also find that focusing on an individual project saves time because you'll remember what you've done so your edits will remain consistent throughout your book. Learn more about using your spelling checker in the information box on the next page.

Note: The hashtags you see in the sidebar boxes in this book are handy little dudes and they are becoming more so now that Twitter and other online entities are using them to lead readers to more detailed information and related conversations. Traditionally, though, public relations people used them to indicate closure at the end of media releases and you'll still see them used to mean "The End" on the last page of manuscripts and other places.

Word's **Spelling and Grammar Checker** is like a good friend. We come to understand it, accept its faults, and love it for what it is. To make it work for you, go to the **Review** tab on your menu bar. Click. Find and click on the **Spelling & Grammar Icon** and then on **Options**. Put checks by the features you feel will be most helpful to you. You will probably want to utilize the **AutoCorrect Options**—again select the ones that will help you the most. I put a checkmark by **Readability Statistics** when I'm writing nonfiction and suggest those who write children's books select it, too. (We'll talk later about what statistics will do for you.) For now, be aware that after you have run a spelling and grammar check, a statistics window pops up that lets you discover details about your writing. Be sure to click the **OK** button at the bottom of the window before closing it.

Note: You may get tired of the Spelling and Grammar Checker habit of stopping at any hint of a passive construction. Resist the temptation to click on the **Ignore All** button. Instead, use each stop as an opportunity to review the entire paragraph for everything from passive voice to wordiness to repetition of the same idea. To help you with this step in your editing process, use the Index in this book to find references to *passive*.

##

CHAPTER THREE
BEST BOOK FORWARD:
GREAT EDITING *IS* GREAT BRANDING

So what does editing have to do with your marketing, or more specifically your branding as an author? When we brand, everything counts. That includes the way you present yourself as *you*. You are the thoroughbred of your writing world. You want your best colors showing.

Many of you reading this book have read *The Frugal Book Promoter* or you have experience in marketing from your day job so you know about branding, but it may be a new term to many. Branding is as important to writers as it is to General Motors or Swisher. If you don't know what Swisher is, then they haven't done a great job of branding—at least not to you. You do have a firm image of Coke whether you drink it or not. Now, those people know branding!

Coke's colors are red and white. Your best colors include not only flawless editing (or as close to flawless as you can possibly come) but the way your edited material is presented. Shoot for superior quality by putting whatever you send out, including preliminary marketing materials like query letters, on good paper and a letterhead that fits with how you want to be perceived as an author, including (if you wish) your own logo. When you use e-mail, it should be as professional as your letterhead—from the subject line to the signature.

You can even save yourself time by automating your e-mail signatures. Using a complete signature in *every* e-mail is only thoughtful. Editors don't want to scrounge around for essential information, but neither does your Aunt Esther who also appreciates that your phone number and Web address are handy. There is more information on signatures in Chapter Eighteen.

Know, too, how to write concise but interest-catching subject lines for your e-mail subject-line window. As an example, use the term *Media Release* not *Press Release* and follow that with a phrase that will compel an editor to open his or her mail. To do that, use strong verbs and, when possible, suggest a tie-in to current or pertinent news.

These niceties are related to writing, marketing, *and* editing. Branding is part of marketing but it's something you've been doing unconsciously since your mother insisted you take a shower and brush your teeth in the morning. They are covered in more detail in the second edition of *The Frugal Book Promoter* along with everything else you need to know to make a great marketing partner for your publisher and publicist. Right now, however, as part of the branding aspect of putting your best book forward—your best *self* forward—order your stationery and explore your e-mail program for the signatures function. E-mail me with AUTOSIGNATURE SAMPLE in the subject line at HoJoNews@AOL.com and I'll send you an example of one way to design your signature at no charge.

SECTION TWO

THE HANDIWORK OF PUBLISHING

CHAPTER FOUR

MANUSCRIPTS—LETTING
THE HARDCOPIES FLY

I divide this book between the kinds of edits best done manually and those you can let your computer help you with. The manual edits ask you to let your instincts and experience do the heavy lifting. The computer edits remind me more of this adaptation of the old yellow-pages motto: "Let your typing fingers do the walking." Because you probably love writing and language more than tech, we'll start with the manual edits. But starting there is *practical*, too. The cleaner your copy, the less likely you (or your computer) are to make mistakes on individual editing processes.

About the time you are ready to click on the reply key to send a query letter or to pop a manuscript in the mail, stop! Here's where the real work starts. It isn't send-off time. It's printout time—real paper, real ink, rested eyes that haven't been staring at a screen all day. Every document that leaves your desk deserves a manual edit. I prefer to edit twice or, as your doctor is fond of saying, "As often as needed." That way, when I begin to edit onscreen I have fewer errors to spot.

Even though this manual edit is a hardcopy edit—not a new draft or a revision—I make every correction I see then and there, even if I run across something I know the computer will help me pick up later. Spelling. Grammar. Typos. Dialogue tags. Maybe revisions like organization or structure. If I notice major problems, I go back to the computer to fix them immediately rather than wait until I'm though reading the document. I don't believe in saving up corrections until the very last pass through a manuscript. This includes formatting tweaks, which are traditionally thought of as the job of the publisher.

Speaking of editing surprises, you might get a big one when galleys (printed proofs) appear in your mailbox. They arrive just when you think you are published, when you think you can kick back and breathe. No. Instead, you become the editor of your *publisher's* formatting booboos—those errors that occur in the process of making all the edits you didn't. When you see the galley (or the proof copy) of your book, your job is not simply one of accepting or rejecting edits but to check up on any other errors that have occurred. You want to make this galley edit easier by turning in a whistle-clean manuscript—right now— before your book gets to this stage.

Though Post-it notes are a great tool for working with manual edits, I like to use white mailing labels leftover from printing projects to tag situations I'll need to work on later. I fold the label over the edge of the page and make a note on it, then take my time to write what changes I had in mind on that specific hardcopy page. My handwriting has been known to get sloppy and, when it does, I might not fully understand the edit I intended several days ago. That's another trick the gremlins use. I suspect they own wands that induce senile moments. They can also sense your lax moments, your tired times. They'll even know when you decide to sip a glass of wine as you edit.

While we are talking nitty-gritty stuff here, my talented writing friend Kathe Gogolewski entered a contest that gave her feedback as part of the entry fee. She was surprised that she had been docked two points for not starting her short story manuscript one-third of the way down the first page. She says, "When you're getting close to the finalist stage [in a contest], a few points can make all the difference." Think of the package we present to agents and publishers as a contest—only with a different kind of prize. That narrow margin between acceptance and rejection can pivot on font or first-page presentation.

SIDEBAR
Save a Tree

Do a tree a favor. During the editing process, print out copies on paper you've recycled from other edits. To do this, put your salvaged reams into your printer tray being careful to put the clean side up or down, depending on your printer's requirements. Your reward for being a good citizen comes when you get to print out your final copy for submission on pristine paper, one side only.

##

CHAPTER FIVE

DANGEROUS CORNERS AHEAD: COVERS AND QUERIES

Next to you, the writer, those who hold the power over the success of your book are publishers, agents, and editors. That includes acquisition editors at publishing houses and feature, business, and other editors of both print and new media. They are the ones who first learn about you in your cover letter, query letter, or proposal. They are the gatekeepers. Gatekeepers know from experience that writers tend to revert to copy that is full of business-ese when they tackle these documents.

Some gatekeepers have a sense of humor about this and others are not so generous. You will learn in Chapter Eight ("Peeking into the Minds and Query Boxes of Literary Agents") some of the things that most test their patience. Until then you need to know how to avoid that overblown formality they so dread.

Because your introductions to professionals in the industry are so important, these short documents should be edited first in hardcopy just as manuscripts are. Avoid excessive adjectives and self-assessments. In introductory documents *awesome* is a four-letter word. Wordiness, too. Ditch words like *literally* and *virtually* and anything else that sounds stiff or phony.

Stay away from words based in Latin with lots of syllables. It isn't only the long ones that make you sound as if you have no personality, never took a writing class, or are not a publishing professional. So your book is *titled*, not *entitled*. You *live* somewhere, you don't *reside*. You *buy* a book when you're talking to your neighbor. Why suddenly flaunt the word *purchase*? In a TV interview, Meg Ryan was asked what word she loved. She screwed up her face as only she knows how and turned the question around. She said she hated the word *enjoy*. "What's wrong with *liked* or *loved*?" she said. Who would have guessed? This anecdote shows that we can't avoid everything that makes every editor (or actor) peevish, but we can try.

The whole publishing world dislikes the term *fictional novel*. Novels, by definition, are fiction. A lead sentence that says, "I am hoping you will take a look at my fictional novel" is a dull lead, so that makes two strikes against you in one sentence. (Actually three. You don't need *am* or that *ing* word, but we'll talk about those later.) On the other hand, if your story is based on real life, you might say it is a "fictionalized true story," though, you could probably produce more interest with a little more detail, maybe something like, "it's my own story about my life in a Malibu trailer park but I fibbed a lot so let's call it a novel."

We are often told not to be apologetic or self-deprecatory in cover or query letters and, of course, that is true. Avoid saying, "I think" or "I believe." Those phrases weaken your position. Just state what you believe to be the facts. Occasions when an apology is in order are rare. The sample cover letter in Appendix Four of this book gives you an idea of when one might be appropriate. Certainly, never apologize for your book or your credentials.

There is another arcane rule—much ignored—that so narrowly affects our language it is rarely an issue. It *does* affect authors who often work with titles. Let's take *The New York Times*. That's their title and it includes the *The*. So if you were a staff writer reporting on the stylistic independence of that paper, how would you write the lead for your article?

> "Wednesday the *The New York Times* decided to go against practically every stylebook in existence and use *Web site* rather than *Website* within their hallowed pages."

Well, hardly. Using *the* twice looks like a typo. You will encounter this problem often if the title of your book starts with *the*. Ditto for other articles like *a* and *an*.

This is an obscure consideration and therefore grammarians don't hold forth on the subject often. The *Chicago Manual of Style* (bit.ly/ChiStBk) says that when you run across an official title like this in your writing, you put the article in lower case (and you don't italicize it.). So your copy for the release of a title like *The Longest Day of the Year* would read:

> "Simon & Schuster released the *Longest Day of the Year* in January of 2010."

Simon & Schuster might not like that you ignored *the* in the title they took such pains to be sure was just so. If it were your book, you might not much like it either. But that's what occasionally happens when we use a title that begins with an article. The easiest way to solve this problem is to avoid constructions that force you to address it.

The great *Chicago* stylebook doesn't tackle the problem if the title comes first in a sentence because, after all, *The* will be capped by virtue of being the first word in that sentence. Ahh, saved by the easiest grammar rule in any book! But then you must decide whether to keep *The* italicized (because it is part of a title). I couldn't find a source that would even touch that exigency, but I'd italicize it. It seems the problem just went away by rearranging the sentence, so why belabor the point.

Whew! So why did I begin the title of my first book in the HowToDoItFrugally series of books for writers with *the*? ***The Frugal Book Promoter***? Pure ignorance.

You might also wonder why I stuck with a similar title for this book after I knew what a pain that *the* is. I stuck with it because of branding. I discuss branding in more depth in *The Frugal Book Promoter*. It's so important, I discussed it again earlier in this book, because branding's an important thing for us to consider with every step we take in the publishing world—from choosing a title to making sure query and cover letters are edited well. It's about how people perceive you. You're a writer. Like your smile, titles and cover letters are about first impressions. Our smiles, titles, and our names are what people remember *because* we brand them—consciously or subconsciously.

SIDEBAR
Titles Are Tattletales

As long as we're talking about titles, your expertise as a writer will be judged by how you punctuate your titles in any document or e-mail you tuck into an envelope or send on its way.

- A work shorter than a three-act play or a complete book takes (requires!) quotation marks. This includes short stories, essays, songs, poems (other than epics), and one-act plays. It also includes individual chapters from books, articles in periodicals including daily newspapers, and episodes or parts of serials on radio or television.

- Titles of larger works made up of smaller segments including books, three-act plays, movies, the names of newspapers, magazines or journals, and the names of entire television or radio series should be *italicized*. Today that includes the names of blogs (but not individual posts) and the names of Web sites (but not individual pages or articles on that site.)

Cont'd

SIDEBAR
Cont'd: Titles Are Tattletales

Warning! The digital world is changing everything from grammar and spelling to punctuation. E-books and the Internet at large use underlines to designate links, so most editors prefer italics for titles so they won't be mistaken for links.

- Legal documents, the Bible, the Qur'an, the Torah, and other sacred texts do not take quotation marks, underlining, *or* italics. Sometimes a word like "bible" is used in a secular context and is not capitalized.
- Here are the general rules for capitalizing titles: First and last words are capped. So are all other words but the articles (*a, an, the*), conjunctions (words like *and, but, or*), and prepositions of four or fewer letters (worlds like *for, on, off, of*).

  Note: Much disagreement swirls around capping subtitles. The British prefer to cap only the first word in a subtitle. Americans don't. However, Yanks including me are (slowly) taking to this idea, especially since subtitles have grown ever longer to accommodate more keywords to help with online search functions.

  ##

CHAPTER SIX

LET'S MAKE EVERYONE AGREE

We usually think of agreement as it applies to matching up subjects and verbs, but an important manual edit is one that checks to see if plural pronouns match their singular antecedents and vice versa. A few years ago, I coedited *The Complete Writer's Journal* for Red Engine Press (the original publisher for the first edition of this book). Experienced and emerging authors, promoters, and publishers were invited to submit quotations for this journal. It was to include more than one hundred quotations and serve as a gift item, a practical tool for writers, journalers, or sketchers, and be an effort in cross promotion.

I found dozens of these seemingly innocuous agreement errors in these submissions. Some of these entries were so good that my fellow editors and I wanted to use them anyway so we decided to wield our editorial powers to fix them. We sent the edits back to the authors for final approval and I'll be darned if several didn't send their quotations back to us in their original form. My point is that these mismatches are so shifty we don't notice them or we make excuses for them.

Here's an example of a submission we didn't accept: "E-books can be a great promotional tool."

Arguably, the author thought of e-books as a collective term for electronic publishing (and therefore singular). Still it would have been easy to eliminate the ambiguity by making it: "E-books can be great promotional tools" or "E-book technology can be used as a great promotional tool." Of course, you have to identify these possible disagreements before you can edit them.

As you can see, there isn't always only one right way to edit some agreement issues. You have to consider context. If you decide to leave the apparent agreement problem—error or not—dangling out there because you've rationalized it away or because you're just darned stubborn, you might inadvertently cause a gatekeeper to roll her eyes. She may—if she has the time—discover why you made this choice. I can almost guarantee you she won't have the time. Again, when it comes to first impressions, it's better to reconstruct your sentence to avoid the possibility of censure.

Pronoun/antecedent errors are invitations for a professional to judge the writer an amateur. The agreement gremlin knows this. He also knows that in longer sentences they are difficult to spot. They'll often slip by several readers, and that makes him a very happy gremlin indeed.

While you're looking for singulars and plurals, make sure your verbs agree with the true subjects of your sentences. A subject is often disguised by a prepositional phrase lurking in its vicinity. Prepositions (you know—the so-called "position words" like *on, above, between,* and *around* that your fourth grade teacher asked you to memorize) are tattlers that help you avoid identifying objects of prepositions as subjects of sentences.

You may need to refresh your memory because these prepositions aren't really only about position, anyway. Find an extensive list of one- and two- and even three-word (gasp!) prepositions at http://en.wikipedia.org/wiki/List_of_English_prepositions. Keep that address as a favorite but memorize the ones in the one-word group, which isn't long. When you have it memorized, you can more easily identify your true subject to be sure your verb agrees with it.

Speaking of gremlins, your cut-and-paste errors warm the cockles of their little black hearts. So stay tuned. In the next chapter, we'll tackle methods to foil them when you're making these kinds of edits, too.

CHAPTER SEVEN

YOUR CUT-AND-PASTE ERRORS—THE WAY TO A GREMLIN'S HEART

You are sure to use cut-and-paste and copy-and-paste when you revise and edit. This process often leaves behind little telltale letters or words like *be, in, a,* and literally hundreds of other possibilities. They are nourishing meat and potatoes for gremlins and they thrive every time you make a change in your copy.

The worst pieces that get left behind are real words that your spelling checker does not find and your computer's grammar checker might not notice them either. Lurkers like these are the best argument for manual edits.

Cut- and copy-and-paste remnants hang in your copy indefinitely. Only someone else—perhaps a friend who is as detail-oriented as an accountant or (this will become repetitious, I know) a very sharp-eyed editor—can see them. Your earlier writing patterns are part of your subconscious, so you almost certainly will miss at least some of these tiny guys in your own writing. Reread your paste out loud—and the sentence before it and the one after it. Here are a few more tips:

- Check to be sure your paste ends up where you want it. Within a sentence? At the end? A new paragraph?

- When you copy-paste watch for apostrophes and quotation marks. If your source material used straight quotes (") and your book uses curly ("), they will shout "amateur" to gatekeepers.
- When you place your copy cursor in a new document, you get several paste choices. Choose **Use Destination Theme** so the new copy takes on all the formatting choices you've made for your manuscript.
- While you are scouring these leftovers from the cut-and-paste efforts in your last draft, look at your sentences that begin with conjunctions and other connectors like *but, and*, and *so*. Yes, the grammar gurus say you can use these words to begin a sentence, but what if the gatekeeper who gets to vote "Yea" or "Nay" on your precious manuscript doesn't know what you know? You get to choose, but your choice may be different after you've pasted something into your copy. Besides, I wouldn't stake my credibility on starting sentences with conjunctions early in the acceptance game.

By the way, I don't think people who are so techy—people who love to read everything on a screen—are immune to these cut-and-paste errors. In fact it's sometimes the tech-savvy ones who find them the hardest to spot.

CHAPTER EIGHT
PEEKING INTO THE MINDS
AND INBOXES OF LITERARY AGENTS

To avoid tipping off an editor or agent that you are not (yet) a professional (or accidentally leading one to believe you aren't a professional when you are), you must know what ticks them off. When I put out a call for agents' pet peeves, I was overwhelmed by the number of generous agents who were willing to take time to help me help *you*. Many who helped didn't care to be mentioned and so had little to gain from their generosity.

In this chapter I mention those agents who gave me permission to use their names. I also list their contact information in Appendix Three in case you want to send them a query for representation. To tailor your query appropriately, you'll need to visit their Web sites so you can respect their individual guidelines, an important courtesy every single agent I interviewed suggested.

Megan C. Atwood, formerly of **Firebrand Literary Agency**, warns against queries for genres agents don't sell. This was the breach of protocol mentioned most frequently by agents in my unofficial survey. Megan is also not keen on blanket submissions and queries that are not personalized. She cautions against the "overuse of adjectives . . . a warning sign that this person is not a strong writer." She advises against submitting a manuscript similar to one you submitted to her earlier and she declined. Apparently agents have longer memories than writers credit them with.

Lisa Ekus-Saffer of **Lisa Ekus Public Relations Co. LLC** wants to know why you are the one to write this book. She expects typewritten queries and says, "I kid you not!" Imagine how hard it would be for an agent if everyone submitted handwritten queries.

Lilly Ghahremani of **Full Circle Literary LLC** says that it's a turnoff when an author presumes too much. She says, "Just like you may not want someone on a first date to say, '*when* we have our kids ...', it's uncomfortable for an agent to hear, 'I can't wait for you to represent my book!'"

Scott Eagan, **Greyhaus Literary Agency**, says, "You get one chance to pitch to me. If I pass, trying to get me to change my mind will never work."

Matt Wagner, **Fresh Books Literary Agency**, offers an example that subsidy- or self-published authors should avoid as if their publishing careers depended on it (which they may). One of the queries he received said, "I self-published my book at Lulu. I haven't marketed it at all yet." His reaction? "Oh, okay, you mean that a previous round of agents passed on your project, which you then haphazardly published, and now you're too lazy to market your book but you think maybe someone else will take it over for you?"

Wagner doesn't want a novel with only twenty thousand words. He says, "Uh, you mean a two-chapter book? Sorry, that's not long enough to be a book."

Michael Larsen of **Michael Larsen–Elizabeth Pomada Literary Agents** suggests authors follow through. He says, "Find out when you should expect to hear from agents and call or write them if you don't." He suggests authors disclose the fact when they submit to more than one agent at a time.

Kae Tienstra, **KT Public Relations & Literary Services**, would like you to get to the point and don't get fancy on her. She points out that getting cute takes forever for a computer to load and doesn't much impress in real time either. That is seconded by many, including **Liz Trupin-Pulli** of **Jet Literary Agency**. To ignore this suggestion because you feel being clever will make you stand out will be an effort in futility.

Tienstra also says that agents can tell when they're being "buttered up." She says, "We know you're impressed with our 'wonderful publishing credentials and vast experience' as agents. But, ya know? We've only been agents for a short time, so who are we kidding here?" Her comment is also a reminder how essential your homework is before you write and send off your query.

Elaine P. English, **PLLC Literary**, says, "My biggest pet peeve is the author who describes his or her work as a 'fictional novel.'" She also will not read a cover, query, or manuscript in anything less than a ten-point font (and many agents are not that generous). Twelve point is standard.

Stephanie Kip Rostan, agent at **Levine/Greenberg Literary Agency, Inc.**, reminds authors not to query "every single agent at our agency." Either use a general submission form when it is provided online, or choose one agent whose biography is a good match for your project. She also says, don't "slavishly follow a query letter template . . . . If you can't write a query letter on your own, I have to be concerned about your ability to write a book. Besides, it's just creepy."

Roberta Brown, **Brown Literary Agency**, cautions against comparing your work to that of another author. She says, "The bestselling author is already published with a following. No editor wants a copycat." Do notice the difference between a market analysis of books in your book proposal where you compare your book to others in its category or genre to saying that you write like William Faulkner.

Jenny Bent, **Trident Media Group**, reminds authors not to send a CD rather than a manuscript unless the agent specifically suggests it. She also warns against authors sending random chapters when she requested the first three consecutive chapters.

Jeff Kleinman of **Folio Literary Management** says:

- It is presumptuous for authors to ask agents for feedback. He acknowledges they might get some from agents, but not to ask.
- Authors should avoid promising an instant bestseller.
- An author's ability to pitch his book well has "more to do with [the author's] knowing the project is ready to go" than it does with selling it. That's exactly what this book helps you with.
- An author should avoid appearing defensive, argumentative, or apologetic in her query letter.

Here are comments from two agents that will make you feel that agents have warmer hearts than you ever imagined.

Laurie Abkemeier of **DeFiore and Company** says, "If I can't spot the diamond despite the soot, I'm the one who is making the fatal mistake."

Tamela Hancock Murray of **Hartline Literary Agency** says that after careful consideration of my questions to her she can't "think of anything concrete that will cause me to reject a manuscript that has merit." Ahhh. Bet she finds some diamonds passed over by others, too.

> SIDEBAR
> Tips from the Mouth of an Agent
>
> A blog from the mouth and heart of Agent Kristin Nelson will help you with your search for a literary agent. Read it regularly to help you avoid the kinds of errors that turn agents off. It's at nelsonagency.com/pub-rants/
>
> ##

Though a few agents don't mind, **Michelle Wolfson** of **Wolfson Literary** is among the many who want you to avoid trying to sell her more than one book in any given query letter. She says, that's like bringing on a blind date "your three best friends and any brothers you may have in case I like one of them better." She wants you to choose your best and sell it with everything you've got.

Kristin Nelson of **Nelson Literary Agency LLC** warns against queries that are boring, too general, or inappropriate. She wants a good sum-up of the plot and a unique hook. Some agents are patient, though. She says if a query is formatted improperly, she might request that an author polish it and send it again so she can give it "a fair look."

Nelson also notes on her blog (see the sidebar above) that many authors don't seem to know the difference between a tagline or logline (a brief pitchy synopsis like the ones used on movie posters) and a summary. Taglines are one or two sentences that tell just enough about the story to entice someone to read it—usually ending with a cliffhanger—the best device of all to get readers onboard. I go into detail about how to write one in *The Frugal Book Promoter,* but for now, know loglines or taglines are two sentences long and written in present tense using active, strong verbs.

To grasp the idea of a summary, think about the *Cliff Notes* series. A retelling of the story is in order. It isn't a chapter-by-chapter synopsis, but it does hit all the major points. Include the theme or themes. The premise. The hook. The plot points. Subplots or secondary threads. Don't try to hide what happens at the end. You end up with a few paragraphs similar to what you see in a *New York Times*-style review, but one that *does* end with a spoiler and one that *doesn't* critique the work like professional reviews do.

Agents read summaries to decide if they want to read your submitted chapters or entire manuscript. If you have trouble with a summary, go back to your book for another revision and more reading (or classes) in structure. That goes for nonfiction as well as fiction.

Here are suggestions from some of the agents I interviewed who preferred not to be identified:

- Don't start a query with a question. They appear clichéd or at least forced.
- Who you are as a writer impresses some far more than a rundown on the "twists and turns of your book." Remember when you first realized that a blow-by-blow account of a movie bored your parents? It's true with books, too. When space is limited, your plot should be a mere logline, pitch, or teaser. Your credentials or experience will be far more impressive to an agent or publisher.
- Don't cold-call on the phone. Most of the agents I contacted prefer to be warmed up with a query letter. Some prefer no calls. Ever.
- Don't use mass e-mail submission services unless the service will tailor each query to the individual agent being contacted. If you use a service like this, the person you hire to do it should be professional and leave no clues that the person submitting isn't you. Yes, I know some agents will hate that I'm giving you this advice, but some authors do have day jobs, families, and the next book to write.

What advice do agents have that apply to manuscripts as well as queries? **Gina Panettieri** of **Talcott Notch Literary** reminds us:

- Authors should not overuse sentence fragments as a style element.
- Authors who "overuse exclamation points . . . make their books sound as if they were written by a yappy Chihuahua on speed." So there you have it. You'll hear it from me later, but this

time you get it directly from the mouth of an agent.

- A "lack of complete page headers on a manuscript can be a disaster for an agent" who might be working with a dozen manuscripts or more at one time.
- A "manuscript that lacks proper indentations for paragraphs is often too frustrating to read."

Jenoyne Adams, associate agent for **Levine/Greenberg Literary Agency, Inc.**, emphasizes doing a complete rewrite when it is suggested. Patching up a book in "less than three days almost always demands a rejection." She also likes an author to make sure the story begins long before page fifty. She says, "Save the backstory for your research notebook."

I loved that **Larry Kirshbaum** of **LJK Literary Management** gave me another reason (without prompting!) to encourage you to read the first book in my HowToDoItFrugally series, *The Frugal Book Promoter*. He said, ". . . the author must have some kind of important biographical items that can lead to publicity and promotion." He's talking about *platform* or the ability to show an agent or publisher that you are capable of collaborating in the marketing part of publishing a book.

Terrie Wolf at **AKA Literary** recommends my booklet *The Great First-Impression Book Proposal* (bit.ly/BookProposals) for authors to read before they submit a book proposal. If you write nonfiction, you will probably submit a book proposal to an agent before you write the book. If you write fiction or memoir, your agent might not ask you for a book proposal.

If she does, you don't need to read several books to learn to write one. That's why I wrote this little book on proposals—so you can get the information you need in thirty minutes or less. In fact, when (if) your agent asks for a proposal and you have purchased this book rather than borrowing it, e-mail me and I'll send you an e-copy of *Great Impression Book Proposal* at no charge. It's easy. You're on the honor system. If you buy the little paperback on Amazon, you can get the e-copy free as part of their MatchBook feature. Either way, it's an easy way to learn everything you need to know about book proposals—fast.

This list of agents' suggestions does not—cannot—predict every exigency for every title in the entire lexicon of book ideas. It is a list sent to you from the hearts of agents who care. Creativity counts, too, as long as it is integral to making you and your book better understood, not just frou-frou. Enough said, except for one piece of advice from Megan Atwood not to take a rejection personally: "There have been several manuscripts I've had to pass on . . . but I loved them. That is always heartbreaking." As I read her comment, I thought it was a plea not to give up. Keep submitting but also keep improving your craft.

As authors, we need to understand more about agenting (and publishing). We need to work up a little compassion. Agents have businesses to run. They know their contacts. They know which books are likely to sell to those contacts. Only the agent knows his or her own track record, knows his or her other clients, can see how your book fits into his or her mix. If you've written well and done your homework, you and an agent will click.

Having said all this, I am going to tell you something many agents will hate (but also understand). You may ignore the submission guidelines that require you to submit *exclusively*. That goes for submissions to agents, publishers, review journals, anthologies, magazines, and contests. I know because when I was getting started as a professional writer, I attended a conference called Summer Literary Semesters at Herzen University in St. Petersburg, Russia. Editors from some of the most prestigious literary journals in the US sat on one of the panels. One of them said, "Ignore that [exclusivity] rule. Even though we know it is to our advantage, we all also know it is patently unfair to authors." Those were not his exact words; his exact words were considerably stronger. The other panelists all laughed and nodded. I didn't laugh. I applauded. And took notes. Some of us could die of natural causes waiting for back-to-back readings.

If you decide to submit your manuscript to several publishers or agents at once, include that information in the cover or query letter, as agent Michael Larsen suggests. If you are uncomfortable with that, at the very least, track your submissions and let the unlucky (or slower) editors know when another elects to publish your article, story, or book. We authors can refuse to participate in something that does not benefit us in any way, but we should still be as considerate as possible.

Next, let's ignore the naysayers who diss the editing help that computers can give you. That help can be far too valuable to ignore. Instead, we'll work on how you can become a team to come up with the best edited manuscript ever.

SECTION THREE

LET YOUR COMPUTER DO WHAT IT DOES BEST

CHAPTER NINE
USE WORD'S TOOLS—DON'T TRUST THEM

Many editors and writing teachers warn authors against using Microsoft Word tools for editing. That is understandable. They see writers let tools usurp craft. They see how the problems Word's tools cause the unwary outweigh their usefulness. Many editors like Dr. Bob Rich (bobswriting.com/editing.html) advise people to "just turn the grammar checker off."

Though I don't consider myself a techy, I use these dreaded tools because they can be timesavers. To me frugal of time is about the same as frugal with money. You might already know how to make your word processor's tools work for you or feel it is valuable to learn. Over the years I published books almost every way imaginable from doing it the traditional way to doing everything (and I mean everything!) myself. During this painful (and joyful) process, I learned some tool-tricks for avoiding the gaffes that leave smiles on gremlins' faces.

A note of caution before you embark on letting a computer help you with your editing. Use it as a tool sometime *after* your first hardcopy edit and *before* your final edit or *complete reading*. That way if the computer does something unexpected with your copy, you'll see the errors before anyone else does. I promise you, you won't regret this final read. You'll even find a few booboos you won't be able to blame on the computer.

You're an author. You get to change your mind. Lucky you. You have a computer to help you when you do change your mind—either midstream or when you finally type "The End" or put hash marks (##) at the end of your manuscript to let some editor somewhere know this is it! *This* is what they're going to get.

Fiction writers often use the name of a real person to model a character in a story. Then, as they are editing, they come up with a name that is more suitable. Leora Krygier, author of *When She Sleeps*, found it necessary to change the names of her characters twice midstream in the writing process.

> **Warning**: "Your way," is not necessarily the "right way" and vice versa. Sometimes we must make style *choices*. After careful consideration or research you choose to call a bar *Ye Olde Taverne* and, yes, spell it that way. Or you may decide to spell the pages about your book that you keep on the Web *website* or *Website* even though the venerable *New York Times* chooses *Web site*. That's your prerogative, but choices that capitalize Web will be more acceptable to gatekeepers. After making your selection, what you don't want to do is automate your edits to the point where every *old* in your copy comes up *Olde* or where every *site* in your copy gets changed to *Website*. You also don't want these style choices to toggle back and forward between your first choice, second, or third. That becomes downright annoying or confusing to the reader.''

Changes like these usually require beginning-to-end manual edits to be sure that any variations that occur are intentional. This chapter gives you some of my favorite tools (and some not-so-favorite ones) for making these changes when you run across a variation you don't want. You'll see that I keep cautioning you against using Word's Replace All tool. It is powerful, but it can also cause you big headaches. It's probably a no-no to be repetitive but I, too, am a writer and get to make style choices—even content choices. I choose to be repetitive rather than have you come away from this book not remembering that I warned you.

CONSIDER THE SOURCE: TRACK EVERY EDITOR'S SUGGESTIONS

Any critique partner—a professional or someone who agrees to play the part of your typical reader—can be valuable in assessing your work. Each is valuable in a different way. The best way to use these resources is to track corrections and changes rather than making changes willy-nilly as suggestions are made.

In other words, you'll almost always want to evaluate the *source* of criticism before you alter your manuscript. Some critiquers have more expertise than others. You want to know if a particular question or suggestion comes up more than once. The more frequently you hear a criticism or question, the more heavily you weigh it. That's as important in the editing process as it is in a critique group.

Because my handwriting is lousy and because using Word's tracker makes it easy for the author to accept or reject edits, I use it whether I am editing for myself or for someone else. Click. Click. The edit is in or it's out! (For information on how this works, see the next sidebar). If you hire an editor who works electronically, you may ask him or her to do the same for you. Tracker also makes it easy for you to keep a record of suggestions for you to refer back to. Instructions for tracking edits and ideas are in the box on the next page.

Here are some of the ways I use Track:

- To edit my own material when I want to know later what is new and what is old. For more on avoiding picking up a wrong file, refer to Chapter Two under "Avoiding computer confusion."
- When I have an idea I want to use but have yet to rate its brilliance quotient.
- So I can trace whom to credit for quotations or suggestions.
- When I reassemble or edit a second or revised edition of a how-to or textbook, it helps me distinguish new copy from old.
- To help me ascertain whether new information I add repeats what was in the work before. (I address other ways to determine if you've been repetitive later in this section. Check the "Editing Elixir" sidebar later in this chapter, too.)

> **Note:** Repetition is sometimes needed, even intentional. And it's sometimes superfluous. You may know better than your editor which of these categories it falls into once it has been identified.

SIDEBAR
Track Edits and Ideas

See the little tab that says **Review** above the ribbon at the top of your Word screen? Click on it and find the icon that says **Track Changes** where you'll also find a dropdown arrow. You'll find choices under **Change Tracking Options** that allow you to use colored fonts and colored edit balloons to tell you what is new, what is deleted, even what kind of formatting changes get made. You'll also get to assign a different name to each of the colors so you know who made a suggestion and can judge its reliability accordingly. You could let different advisors use different copies or files of your document or you could let them all use the same one—each coded with a different color. When you use Tracker, you can see the original copy right next to the edited copy and decide whether to accept or reject with a right-click and a tap on your mouse.

Note: The toolbar on which you find Tracker must be active. When it isn't active, the icons are faded. To use Tracker, your document must also be in the unprotected mode. To benefit from all the possibilities Tracker offers, click on Tracker's option link.

##

WORD'S UNCRITICAL, UNDISCERNING, BUT THOROUGH EDITING TOOL

Once you finish your manual edits and are back to working on your computer, make corrections as you would when you are writing a first draft. You are working on the computer, but you're essentially making corrections by hand. You can also use Word's powerful gremlin fighter, the Find Function. Use caution; if you get swept away with its magic properties, gremlins will appropriate it, and you might end up with more problems than you had when you started. So, keep it simple and don't get fast and furious with the Replace All button.

Among other things, your Find button can:

- Help eliminate repetitive words and phrases. Use Word's Thesaurus and Synonyms tools to help you add variety or to find a more precise word than your first choice.
- Individualize a specific character's speech pattern by intentionally using repetitive words (very subtly, please!), grammar-specific constructions or slang preferences. (See Chapter Thirteen for more on the subject of dialogue.)
- Eliminate overblown, redundant, and overused adjectives when you don't have a specific reason in mind—words like *awesome* and *great*.
- Eliminate ineffective adverbs.
- Strengthen verbs. As an example, let Word find all the iterations for the often-used and very weak verb *to be* to see if you can find a more active or image-provoking verb.
- Identify passive voice and eliminate it when appropriate. We'll cover how you can use

Readability scores available in Word to help you with this editing process later.

- Rename a character or place or correct an error you know you've made in several places.

The specifics for using the Find Function are in the next information box. Once you are a proficient Find Function user and as your title puts special demands on your editing process, you might think of new uses on your own. Let me know about them. We'll share them as tips or articles in my *SharingwithWriters* newsletter to help other authors with their editing.

You can also use Word's Dictionary with its associated Readability Statistics feature and a professional program called Concordance to help you with some of these tasks. To pursue those avenues, read the information boxes on the next few pages.

SIDEBAR
The ABCs of Find Function

Here's the easiest and most disaster-proof way to use your Find Function:

- When you've clicked on the **Home** tab above the icon ribbon at the top of your Word page, an editing panel appears. The Home tab is usually at the far left of your screen unless your eight-year old has diddled with your Word settings. In that panel, you'll see several editing functions (usually on the far right) including Find, Replace, and Select.
- Ignore Replace. Use only your **Find** function.

Cont'd

- Type in whatever you are trying to find into the window. To avoid finding words you don't want to change, use spaces to isolate the computer's search. **Example**: To find the word *is,* type (space)is(space). That will keep your detail-oriented program from picking up the letters *i* and *s* in every word where they appear together, words such as *list*. As a double check, run a second check on groups of three or four letters to be sure that all the changes were made. If you're changing the name *Christy*, to something else, you might run a find on (space)Chris and isty(space). And then again on the *isty* that includes a period after the *y* (and then again with a comma after the *y*). You'll have your final manual edit to find errors, too.

  Note: Even the (space)word(space) technique will miss some words that are followed by some kind of punctuation. To be thorough use searches like (space)word(comma), (space)word(period), etc. or cue the find function to search for "Whole words Only." To do so, click on the **Options** button in the popup window and explore the possibilities there.

- Make the changes your computer finds one at a time, checking each one you make before you go to the next. Do not rush.

  Note: Using the **Replace** function is a lot trickier. Some professional editors like Dr. Rich, the editor I mentioned before, use advanced functions for global replacements like Match Case, Use Whole Words Only, and Use Wildcards, but I advise most inexperienced authors not to try it.

##

SIDEBAR
An Editing Elixir for the Computer Savvy

Concordance is a computer program that lets you analyze your documents. Those who study or analyze the Bible often use it. You can see examples of how the program is used by those who study literature and to get ideas for your own editing process at dundee.ac.uk/english/wics/wics.htm

Joyce Faulkner, book designer at redenginepress.com, says, "Concordance finds frequently used words so you can determine if they're used too often. You can do this manually, but this program is more accurate and a timesaver." It is a valuable tool for editors and self- and subsidy-publishers who are computer savvy enough to tackle a new program, and it can do much to refine the editing process, including:

- Make indexes and wordlists.
- Count word frequency.
- Compare different uses of a word.
- Analyze keywords for the looming task of marketing your book.
- Find phrases and idioms.
- Pick out jargon that can be improved by using terms more understandable by the masses.
- Publish to the Web.

To buy the program, go to concordancesoftware.co.uk/buynow.htm

##

EXTRA SPACES ARE LIKE FLUFF BALLS UNDER THE BED

You won't be able to see the extra spaces in your copy if you haven't set your word processing program to show the formatting symbols. I usually work with them showing, because many things—like places where we typed in extra spaces—are like fuzzy-wuzzies under the bed. If you don't go to the extra work of getting down on your knees to look for them, you won't see them.

> **Note**: To turn your formatting symbols on so you can see where you have tapped the space bar too often, click on your **File** tab, then on **Options**, then **Display**, and then select all the symbols you want to see. I choose them all, but to find only extra spaces, put a check by **Spaces** for sure. Each space appears as a dot wherever you pressed your spacebar. Don't panic when little paragraph marks (¶) and dots appear all over your pages. You can get rid of them by reversing the process for making them appear.

Getting rid of extra spaces makes it easier for an editor to spot wayward errors and easier for a formatter to make your pages look spiffy.

You can eliminate those spaces one at a time (hours of work in a manuscript of considerable length). If you learned to type back in the dark ages, you can *relearn* to type using only one space between sentences (a headache to say the least). Or you can—carefully—use the **Replace All** feature in your Word program.

Yes, I know I warned you against using the Replace window. I'm saying, "just this *one* time, for just this *one* little clean-up job." Using Replace to dust off the cobwebs is a breeze and very safe compared to the replace functions that some writers use it for. The process for getting rid of extra spaces is a little like using Endust. It picks up most of the small, less-evident particles in your copy and it does it fast.

Slim those chubby spaces between sentences

If you learned to type on an old-fashioned typewriter as I did, you probably still tap the spacebar twice between sentences. Computers do something called *kerning* for you these days. Kerning is the process of proportionately spacing wide and narrow letters on the page so no second tap at the end of a sentence is necessary. Except for those writing their dissertations or other academic work, the battle cry is "Only one space dot between sentences, please!" Even those of you who learned to keyboard recently will probably pick up an occasional stray extra space when you do your manual edit. Using the method in the next sidebar will keep you from getting eyestrain watching for them.

Eliminate pesky extra spaces at the end of paragraphs

Let's start with the spaces we stick into our copy before we push the spacebar to start a new paragraph. We do this because it feels like—because it is—the end of a sentence as well as the beginning of a new paragraph.

After you've set up your Word program to show you where the spaces are, delete the little dots you find at the end of every paragraph—dots other than periods or other punctuation. Go back through the entire document. Inspect the end of every paragraph. Take out the *one* you see there (there will probably only be *one*) by using your backspace key to delete it.

SIDEBAR
Let Your Replace Function Spot the Dots

Select your **Home tab**. Find the editing section of Word's ribbon and click on **Replace**. When you click, you find two windows.

- Tap your **Spacebar** twice in the first window that says **Find what**. It will appear as if you have typed nothing.
- In the next window labeled **Replace with**, tap the **Spacebar** only once. It, too, will look as if there is nothing there.
- Now glance down to the bottom of the pop-up rectangle to find a selection of buttons. Find **Replace All**. Click. Voilà! Even with two apparently blank windows, you will send a message to your computer's brain to replace all the double spacing in your document—whether between words or between sentences—with single spacing.

Cont'd

SIDEBAR
Cont'd: Let Your Replace Function Spot the Dots

Caution: Before you tap your **Spacebar** in both the **Find what** and **Replace with** windows, be sure your **cursor** is as far to the left of each little window provided for you to type in your replacements as it can go. To do that, backspace until the cursor bar can go no farther left before entering your invisible spaces.

Now peek. You should see no double spaces at the end of any of your sentences. Some extra cautious types (me?) repeat the function just in case there are places I've accidentally typed three spaces. It seems there are always a few additional spaces for Word to erase for me.

##

A quick aside, frugally speaking. If you are self-publishing, the formatter you hire might give you a price break if you tell him or her that you have done some of the preliminaries yourself including dusting out double spaces.

YOUR UNTRUSTWORTHY SPELLING AND GRAMMAR CHECK

The Spelling and Grammar check on your computer is an important helper. Because it is in cahoots with the gremlins, you need to do a complete Spelling and Grammar run when you start your first edits and again just before you do your last *manual* edit. You find the checker in the Ribbon of your Word program near an icon showing ABC and a blue checkmark. You probably turned yours on or set it to active mode during the preliminary edit. A few authors find checkers an intrusion on their writing process. Even those who trust their own skills more than they do the automated checker (and they should) will want to run documents through final checks. If you aren't proficient in Word, you'll find how to do it in "Sidebar: Your Flawed Friend" in Chapter Two.

A thorough check will help you revaluate lots of nitty-gritties in your document. It is excellent at some things like the correct plural spellings of nouns that end in *o* like *avocado*. Should the plural end in *es* or plain old *s*? This is one thing it knows for sure.

The spelling checker will pause where its computer brain thinks there is a spelling or grammar error. You choose to accept its suggestion or not. Here are some reminders that will make the task easier:

- This computer function isn't an editor and it won't sense as many errors as you'd think its little automated brain should. It will be up to you to fine-tune your document—and then fine-tune it again.

- Read the prompt at the top of the window that appears on your screen as the checker finds questionable spots. It tells you *why* it has selected the passage. If you neglect that little indicator, you might not understand why the computer stopped there and correct for something else, or—just as bad—assume all is well with what you are looking at.

- Don't let yourself get too tired. If this exercise becomes perfunctory, the gremlins will seize the advantage.

- Resist the temptation to keep clicking on the **Ignore** button. Checker highlights so many things that you absolutely, 100% *know* you must ignore that you begin to click without thinking. Each selection is a red flag. A Band-Aid. Check the grammatical term in the prompt box every time. If you're unsure, look it up in your grammar resources. Keep a running tab of its suggestions that puzzle you (copy and paste them into a separate file) and run them by your editor once you have one.

Your Spelling and Grammar Checker, after all, is a computer program. It might make your little booboos less likely to turn into infections. For it to be an antibiotic that doesn't lose its potency from overuse, let it point out possible trouble and then make up your mind about the validity of anything it finds. If you find it pointing to a style choice you make frequently (say, beginning your sentences with conjunctions), that's your cue to decide if your *ands* and *buts* have become annoying and edit *some* or *all* of them out.

YOUR CUSTOM DICTIONARY: MAKING IT PERSONAL

Word is designed to serve as many needs as possible. That's one of its beauties and one of the things that makes it difficult to use. Not so its Custom Dictionary tool. It's yours to use for whatever purpose you need it. It is there when you're making up your own words, interpreting the sounds of a dialect, and assuring the correct spelling of place names or people's names. It's there when you're using the jargon that often accompanies niche market business books (though I encourage authors of these kinds of books to simplify jargon for easier reading and to help broaden their readership). I considered using it to accommodate Utah's regional vocabulary in my fiction but found a few other ways to make the unique vocabulary there work without it.

Go to your **File** tab, then click on **Proofing** and then **Custom Dictionaries**. You'll find languages there but you'll also find places to add about anything else you want to your dictionary.

> **Note**: If you're curious about the techniques for clarifying regional or foreign vocabularies or language, study *The Kite Runner* (bit.ly/HosseinisLangTech). Khaled Hosseini is a master at it. Learning to do this well is the tiniest niche within a niche ever, but Hosseini could write an entire book on how to do it—and probably should.

Oh, and about those style choices I told you that you might have to make. If they're firm spelling choices, you can add them to your custom dictionary. If they are discipline-specific spelling choices, use a search engine to get a feel for what that specific industry considers correct, or get input from an expert in the field before you let Word make your choice permanent in its little digital head.

If you need specific help to make Word's dictionary work for you, the next information boxes may clarify details for you.

The dictionary that comes with your Word program can be changed to include words that it doesn't know or style choices that it doesn't consider. When you're doing a Spelling and Grammar Check, you will be given the option to add an alternative to the dictionary that comes installed in Word. Just know that whatever you add there becomes a permanent part of your dictionary until you choose to purge it.

Note: Word lets you create up to ten dictionaries for your own needs. Using a separate custom dictionary of your own for, say, tech words or style choices is safer than incorporating them into your major dictionary. If you do that and want to go back to writing a book for the general public, your computer won't alert you to the Webby or techy changes you've made.

Here are three examples of changes that might be better used in one of your custom dictionaries than instituted into your program's main dictionary.
- You want a name like *Karen* to be spelled *Karren* and don't want to get a red squiggle every time you use it that way.
- You make up words or names that you expect to repeat. Place names are often disguised to achieve anonymity.
- You are using misspellings to indicate dialect. You spell "sez" for *says* and you don't want to confuse your reader by sometimes spelling it "sayz."

Cont'd

SIDEBAR
Cont'd: Playing with Word's Dictionary

- You are writing for the Web and don't want to be reminded of traditional spelling and grammar for certain things like the overuse of exclamation points or initialism like LOL and OMG. Note that if you get too cute with anything from emoticons to punctuation—even on the Web—you might be setting yourself up for criticism from the grammar cops. That's worrisome if you are trying to forge a literary career.

- James Patterson might use the Readability Statistics feature (more on this feature later in this chapter) to keep his paragraphs no more than two sentences in length. In other words, this tool can help you with certain aspects of pacing your story and keeping the pages open and readable.

- I use Readability Statistics in Word's Dictionary to see what percent of my copy is in passive construction. I sure don't want my readers taking a snooze. When the passive construction percentage is worrisome, we can go back and work on active construction—and, while we're at it—the strength of our verbs.

   Note: Set your Spelling and Grammar Checker to include grammar and presto! It will automatically alert you to specific instances of passive construction in your document. Learn more about passives in Chapter Twelve.

Cont'd

SIDEBAR
Cont'd: Playing with Word's Dictionary

Learn more about the Custom Dictionaries at kerryr.net/webwriting/tools_custom-dicts.htm.

Another Microsoft tutorial gives you tips to eliminate changes you've made to your Word Dictionary—on purpose or accidentally. Go to support.microsoft.com/kb/86557.

For other custom dictionary recommendations, see Appendix Two of this book. To find still more, Google *custom dictionary* + (use the plus symbol) and then type the subject you are looking for after the plus sign. Readymade science, jargon, and dialect dictionaries are available as books and as computer programs.

Reminder: Occasionally Word kicks out a misspelled word that you are sure you spelled correctly. Do your own research even if it seems as if it's a waste of time. Word could be wrong, but so could you.

LET READABILITY STATISTICS AND WORD COUNTS KEEP YOU ON YOUR TOES

I worry that the word *statistics* encourages authors to avoid using Word's readability feature, because most writers need statistics even if they hate them. We *need* word count to make our documents (text) fit an editor's space requirements. We *need* page counts to judge how expensively (or frugally) they can be printed. Here are a few other important uses for statistics:

- Young adult (YA), children's book authors, and educators use Readability Statistics to target a specific grade level. With no extra effort, statistics inform you of the education level of your copy. The tool bases this assessment on a whole series of essentials from vocabulary difficulty to sentence structure.
- Journalists and freelancers use it to keep their copy within the reading range of a periodical's audience. Freelancers won't be surprised that some newspapers want their copy aimed at about fourth grade reading level.
- Instructions for accessing Readability Statistics are in the information box on the next page.

To access your document's statistics in Word 2010, click the **File** tab, then **Options**, then **Proofing**. Go down to where the program asks you to check preferences for the **Spelling and Grammar**.

When you select Readability Statistics (that is, put a check in the box next to those words), the statistics automatically appear each time you reach the end of Word's spell checking process.

##

YOUR OWN STYLE GUIDE

Earlier in this chapter we talked about style choices. Sometimes you'll follow the suggestions of a style guide. Other times you'll make choices based only on your artistic instincts and the needs of your readers. Either way, you'll thank yourself if you start a separate document to record your choices, especially when you are writing a long manuscript. Because a do-it-yourself style guide is more focused, you won't have to play search-and-find games to spot similar entries earlier in your document, in Word's dictionary, or in a custom dictionary.

Don't deviate too far from accepted practices for any genre or project when you make choices. Like making medical decisions, it is smart to get several opinions when stylebooks disagree, but consider the specialty or focus of the stylebook, too. If you're writing books, give preference to *Chicago Manual of Style* (bit.ly/ChiStBk). You might also want to compare its suggestions to *Garner's Modern American Usage* (bit.ly/USAUsage) if your write for the US market. If you write in several genres or for several different media, you need two (or more!) different style guides. Check Appendix Two under "Grammar and Style" for the ones that fit your needs best.

Because I occasionally write for newspapers, I pay attention to their different style choices. What I learn sometimes informs the decisions I make when I'm writing for myself or writing in new genres. *Web site* is an example of a style choice that is yours alone to make. The *Los Angeles Times* and hundreds of publications both online and in print use *website*. I think *Web site* is more accurate because Web is capitalized when it stands alone and *The New York Times,* a trusted model in the US, uses *Web site*. Still, *website* or *Website* are becoming so common that I might soon change my mind.

Remember the political brouhaha around the word *bussing*? Eventually—much to my chagrin—most everyone agreed on *busing* (with one *s*) to mean the practice of moving schoolchildren from one school district to another in the interest of diversification. The latter defies the rules of spelling we all once learned. That is, *busing* should be pronounced *bewsing*, We don't need anything more in our language to confuse the spelling-challenged. You know my mantra, though. Once common usage determines a generally accepted protocol, you don't want to raise the ire of a gatekeeper by going it on your own. Luckily I don't think I'll have to use *busing* in very many of my documents.

For this book, I decided on *e-book* over *ebook*, and *e-mail* over *email*. If *e* stands for *electronic* then it would be *electronic book* or *electronic-book*, not *electronicbook*. That's my stand. You might stand on another platform altogether. Once the big guys make a choice, it is best to go along with it, especially when the acceptance of our work is at stake. It looks as if my position on *e-book* and *e-mail* might be as soundly trounced as the stand I took on *bussing*. Dan Poynter decided to forego the hyphen when he founded his Global Ebook Award (globalebookawards.com/). Sometimes frequency trumps what is rational but not necessarily what is acceptable by gatekeepers. Choices can be tough.

Sometimes none of the stylebooks weighs in on the choice that must be made. In this book, *The Frugal Editor*, I decided to capitalize Word's functions and features. So, when I refer to Word's Find Function specifically, I use caps, but not when I speak of find functions in a generic sense. I used the Find Function to go back and make those changes after I made that momentous decision. That's when I ran into trouble. It seems computers don't understand the difference between brands and generic terms—not when they are identical in every way but the capitalization.

But the problem got even stickier. I wanted to put Find Function in bold typeface, but only when you need to apply the function to a specific process. I tell my clients that we don't need to hit our readers over the head with answers. They're smart. Still there's something to be said for clarity, and I thought the bold labels would help with the how-to process. That meant each occurrence of all these terms (and there are a lot of them!) had to be evaluated to see if caps should be used as if they were titles for different functions. Then again to see if bold was called for when they were used specifically as instructions.

Decisions you make regarding your choices for books are more important than some others because the book industry is very traditional and tends to be more structured (critical?) about what it considers "right." As an example, they generally spell out numbers up to one hundred in books unless there is a very good reason not to. A nonfiction book that uses many mathematical formulas might be one of those exceptions. They also make a big deal of using curly quotation marks rather than the straight ones you see so often on the Web.

So back to your own style guide or style sheet. Whatever you decide, record your decision. I like to use Excel for this because it lets users categorize words and phrases and alphabetize them easily, but a separate Word file will work almost as well.

Without a style sheet, you won't remember every choice you made. Style sheets are your best weapon against gremlins and time-wasting searches after your own knowledge of the language you write in.

Speaking of timesavers, there is a sneaky way to avoid researching something you've forgotten but are fairly certain you'll remember later in the next information box.

SIDEBAR
Code Words Served Batman:
They Can Serve You, Too

You can use your own codes to designate an elusive word or concept. It isn't—strictly speaking—one of Word's fancy schmancy editing tools, but it lets Word's power work for you until what you forgot comes back.

- Use any codename. JayCe Crawford couldn't think of the name for an old-time restaurant called DuPar's Deli in Glendale, California. She used *Jerry's* as a substitute. When she finally remembered, she used the Find Function to replace *Jerry's* with *Dupar's*. One of the advantages to this method is that if you never recall the name and can't find it in research, the name you've used as code might do just as well.
- Use a series of XXXs. I prefer this method because:
  - It's easy to see three capital Xs even without any help from a computer.
  - It's easy to run a Find on three Xs.
  - If I should miss making a change, any editor will notice my *faux pas* so we can fix it together.

Of course, the easiest method is to ask your husband or the girl sitting next to you at Starbucks if they can remember the name that eludes you. One question can save lots of time.

###

USING SHORTCUTS FOR THE STUFF WRITERS NEED

When you were a kid, you may have taken shortcuts across vacant lots. You walked the same way so often you wore a barren path along your route. Now you can do the same thing with computer shortcuts without running the risk of having someone yell at you for trespassing or for ruining their lawn.

You'll love Microsoft's AutoCorrect functions and shortcuts just as much.

Magical automatic aids

AutoFormat As You Type function lets you type faster because the computer takes over for you. Example: *The Frugal Editor: Do-it-yourself editing secrets for authors: From your query letter to final manuscript to the marketing of your new bestseller* is a very long title. By storing it in AutoFormat As You Type, I only need type *The Frugal Editor:* and the computer does the rest. It also keeps me from making errors when I type. (Now, *that's* an editing aid I could only dream about in my typewriter days.)

If you're wondering why I use long subtitles in my nonfiction, it's because they increase findability when searches are made using online bookstores' search engines. Findability is important for book sales. When Clinton was writing his book, he might have said, "It's about the *keywords*, stupid!" To know more about marketing your book, find this book's sister, *The Frugal Book Promoter* using Amazon's search feature. It's another book with a very long subtitle.

SIDEBAR
Auto Functions

Auto functions must have been designed by one of Word's techy geniuses. They are one of my favorite power tools because there is very little chance they will turn on you and cooperate with the gremlins. Just test each entry and adjust as needed before you move on to a new task.

To use **AutoFormat As You Type** and **AutoCorrect**, click on your **File** tab. Go down to **Options** and click. Find **Proofing** in the panel of choices you are given and click. At the top of that box find a shaded box that says **AutoCorrect Functions** and click. You'll find three important tabs: **AutoCorrect**, **AutoFormat As You Type** (the one I use for long titles and phrases that I use repeatedly), and **AutoFormat**. Decide which one works best for whatever terms you use frequently. Some automatic formats are already filled in for you.

> **Example**: Under AutoCorrect, you'll see that Word has already fixed it so that if you type (open parentheses)c(close parentheses), the copyright © symbol magically appears. We authors need that one a lot. If you don't want that done for you, however, you can remove it. In other words, you can tailor AutoCorrect to become a list that works on the stuff *you* want it to work on.

Cont'd

To store a long title or phrase easily, type it into Word formatted as you'd most often use it including bold face, italics, punctuation, and font size. **Highligh**t it. Repeat the **File**, **Option**, and **Proofing** steps. Choose **AutoFormat As You Type**. Your phrase shows up in a box and you type in how much of that phrase you want to type before the computer takes over and puts the rest of it into your document. I've never reached a limit for what it can do. I've even used it for short credit lines that go at the end of things like op-ed pieces or articles.

AutoFormat lists several formatting choices. There you'll find the choices for how quotation marks, fractions, and the all-important hyphens and dashes we talk about later should look. All you need to do here is check or uncheck the appropriate ones for the document you're working in.

Note: Publishers of print books are very fussy about their quotation marks and apostrophes If you're writing a book, choose **Curly Quotation** marks in both of the Auto functions that offer that choice and be sure to click **OK** in all three of the windows you opened to do this job. You can choose to use straight quotations for e-books, especially if you have chosen a font like Arial that doesn't use little feet. Also choose **Ordinals spelled out**, unless you book is about tech. Numerals like 2nd look plain silly in a book. I mean, how many characters are you saving anyway?

##

Do-it-yourself shortcuts and symbols

The next few information boxes tell you how to use the Symbol function and also lists a few shortcuts that writers frequently need. Some shortcuts are available in the AutoFormat tool mentioned in the information box above, too, but knowing how to type the ones you use often gives you control and is often just as fast.

SIDEBAR
Best of the Best Shortcuts for Writers

These symbols are usually made using the **Alt** key *and* the **Ctrl** key *and* a **symbol** from the keypad on your regular keyboard or the designated one on your numeral pad which is usually found at the far right end of your keyboard. A few don't require the Alt key.

When both the **Alt** key and the **Ctrl** key are part of the instructions, they must *both* be *held down* while you type in the last prompt.

Memorizing these combinations are great exercises for the brain, almost as good as paying for brain games on Luminosity.com, and they'll speed up your typing process. Here are a few of the ones you might need when you're formatting or want your copy to look professional:

™, **the trademark symbol**: Alt + Ctrl + T
©, **the copyright symbol**: Alt + Ctrl + C

Cont'd

SIDEBAR
Cont'd: Best of the Best Shortcuts for Writers

®, the registered trademark symbol: Alt + Ctrl + R

é, accent mark: Alt + Ctrl + '(apostrophe) and release. Then type in the letter you want to accent to appear over, say, the *e* or *a*.

—, em dash: Alt + Ctrl + the minus sign on the numeral keyboard (more on em dashes in Chapter Fourteen).

–, en dash: Ctrl + the minus sign on the numeral keyboard (more on en dashes in Chapter Fourteen).

-, nonbreaking hyphen: Ctrl + Shift + the underline. (That's the key to right of the zero on your regular keyboard).

> **Note**: The nonbreaking hyphen is used with dates (1912-1918) and in indexes for ranges of pages.

–, the optional hyphen: Ctrl + – (the minus key on your numeral keypad).

> **Note:** You will probably need the optional hyphen only when you are setting type—like when you are trying to avoid gaposis between words in a justified block of type or when you need to break words between syllables, usually at the end of lines. Word normally fixes lines so you don't need to do it yourself. When you do need it, you'll be glad you have it in your tool kit. When you use it, be wary of making any future edits which often force the optional hyphen to do unexpected things to your copy.

##

English borrows words from many languages. Many of those languages use the same alphabet but different symbols and marks to clarify pronunciation. Sometimes those of us who write in English can make style choices not to use those marks, but sometimes our dictionaries retain them as preferred spelling.

For accent marks, umlauts, cédilles, graves, and other marks you need when you're using foreign words in your copy, find the **Insert** tab at the top of your Word screen. Then click on **Symbol** in your ribbon and then select the **typeface** you are using in your copy to get the exact symbol you need. A word like voilà (French) shouldn't be left barren and embarrassed when you can easily put the grave over the *a*. You'll need symbols if you use Spanish and many other languages, and you'll find math symbols, wingdings, and others there, too.

If you *write* in a language that uses different symbols or alphabets, you probably already have your computer set for that language and may even use a different keyboard, but the Symbol tool will still help you keep your copy the way you'd prefer to see it when you use foreign words.

For more on dialectical marks go to french.about.com/od/pronunciation/a/accents.htm.

##

SECTION FOUR

EDITING FOR
STRONGER WRITING

CHAPTER TEN
HUNTING DOWN
YOUR DREADED ADVERBS

You might recall I mentioned that I begin the editing process by dredging up adverbs. You might wonder why in the world-of-writing I would want to search for adverbs which we all know are perfectly good parts of speech, parts used frequently by the most scholarly among us.

They're ugly, that's why. If you never thought of them that way, you will after you've read this chapter. They're often redundant. They cloak weak verbs. In fact, they are probably first cousins to the gremlins we're trying to ban from our existence. Well, OK, that's a little strong because we want to keep some of them, but you get the idea. The good news: You can use your Find Function to root them out. (Review Chapter Nine to keep Word's Find Function headaches to a minimum.)

THE OBVIOUS *LY* ADVERBS

First, let's look for the obvious adverbs, words that end with *ly*. Type ly(space) or ly(period) into your Find window. That space keeps Word focused on what you want to look at. When you find an *ly* adverb, ask yourself: Is this adverb redundant?

For example, "She ran quickly toward the car." The word *run* implies *quickly*. Some of the adverbs you find will not be that blatantly repetitious, but you will see that many adverbs contribute nothing to what would be left if you axed them. You might feel that *quickly* is needed. Perhaps you're making a stronger point than the word *run* achieves on its own. If that's the case, you haven't finished your analysis. The verb itself might be so weak it requires the adverb. By changing to a stronger verb, you strengthen the sentence and eliminate the adverb in one edit.

If no appropriate substitute for that verb comes to you, use the Thesaurus that Word provides for you, or the real live one in that mini library you prepared for the top of your desk (see the list in Chapter Two) or check dictionary.com. Consider *sped*, *rushed*, or *sprinted*. We'll talk about other ways to replace adverbs with more original language in a bit.

Overuse of adverbs (along with the use of too many overblown taglines—those indicators that tell readers who said what) are so offensive that jokes about them have been named Tom Swifties. Maybe you're too young to be familiar with the classic Tom Swift adventures for boys. Maybe you're a girl who never read a Tom Swift book or cares to, but Tom Swifties are one-line jokes lampooning the style of Victor Appleton, the author of the original Tom Swift books. People started making jokes about his overuse of adverbs and the unnecessary taglines he wrote into his dialogue. Like Polish jokes, they were so much fun that a whole series of them became available for the pun- and fun-loving. Appleton, of course, laughed all the way to the bank, but that's a lesson for one of my marketing seminars, not this book on editing.

A single example from one of the Swift books suffices to let you know what to watch for. Thanks to an article by Roy Peter Clark for this:

"'Look!' suddenly exclaimed Ned. 'There's the agent now! . . . I'm going to speak to him!' impulsively declared Ned.'"

Even authors who swear that adverbs are magical descriptives and are reluctant to give up their clever taglines can see how, well . . . awful this is. Some writing that comes to the desks of gatekeepers looks almost as bad. Let's start by axing ineffective adverbs. We'll talk later about tricks for purging many of your taglines and, by doing so, make your writing more descriptive.

IS THIS ADVERB RELATED TO Y'KNOW?

Maybe you have heard *y'know* but never

SIDEBAR
A List of Words That
Might Be Adverbs

Using the Find Function, do an individual search on each word on this list with an eye to your own habits. After a while, you will know your writing routines well enough to narrow the searches to the most likely trouble causers. I starred those used incorrectly or overused most frequently in the editing I do.

almost
always
even*
far
fast
less
maybe
more
never
not
often*

Cont'd

only*

perhaps

really*

sometimes

seldom

soon

then

today

tomorrow

too*

usually

very*

well

yesterday

Remember the find-function trick of isolating your search by typing in a space on both sides of the word you are trying to find. Example: *Even* gets entered as (space)even(space).

##

thought of it as an editing problem. We know the phrase is related to repeating "uh" in a speech when we are nervous. They tell us at Toastmasters that we must get rid of this affliction. But some of us use adverbs the same way—filler. We stick them into our copy for no other reason than it mimics the way we think or talk, but y'know, I really hate that, and an agent or editor is going to . . . y'know . . . hate it even worse. Even if these filler-words are part of dialogue, you want to use them sparingly. Though using speech patterns to help delineate characters can be a useful tool, more than a hint of an annoying verbal trait can tire your readers or unintentionally become laughable.

Your *ly* search will bring up many words in the y'know category really frequently. So, do you really need it? If you are a fiction writer and *really* is part of the speech pattern of your fourteen-year-old valley girl, you might want to spot a *really* here and there, but do trim them somewhat so they don't become so annoying they take your reader out of the story. If not—and there is no other real . . . oh, no!—good reason for keeping them, be honest with yourself and eliminate them. Consider each—one by one—and be tough. Repetitive words are not jewels to be treasured. One of the beauties of the English language is that we have a huge vocabulary list to choose from.

Editing your idiosyncratic adverbs

As you know, adverbs do not always end in *ly*. The ones that don't are the more dangerous ones. They aren't as easy to spot and we tend to overuse them in speech.

Though a find function is not a therapist, yours can help you with your personal oddities. I overuse *just*. *A Cup of Comfort* author JayCe Crawford watches for *euphemistically*, of all things. Use your find feature and evaluate your favorites in terms of both frequency and effectiveness. Don't let your attachment to these words keep you from using the delete button. Your editor— the one provided by your publisher or the one you hire (unless you're being stubborn or . . . er, inordinately frugal)—will not be as familiar with your writing eccentricities as you are if you have analyzed your own writing patterns.

If you do need a therapist to spot the words your subconscious loves, consider buying the Concordance program I mentioned before. It will spot any word you overuse—not just adverbs. If you work with a vocabulary of your own—a dialect, an accent, or jargon—create a custom dictionary in Word to be sure you aren't overusing a word or to help you regularize the spelling of a word you've made up so that it doesn't vary throughout your manuscript. (See the sidebar in Chapter Nine for help with custom dictionaries and Appendix Two for recommended reading and resources.)

To find the adverb culprits that do *not* end in *ly*, do a search on each individual adverb in the "List of Words that Might Be Adverbs" in the sidebars earlier in this chapter.

> **Note**: While you're doing this massive check, run a find on *as well as* (all three words used together), *too*, and *also* for redundancy. Writers often use more than one of these in a single paragraph or even a single sentence when only one is needed. Sometimes none is needed because the context makes the concept of *in addition to* clear.

DOES THIS ADVERB MAKE YOUR VERBS LOOK SILLY?

You have probably seen those often-humorous lists of sentences where adverbs split infinitives or where they modify the wrong word, idea, or phrase. To avoid humiliation, it is a good idea to go back over your entire document to assess adverbial placement after you've cleansed your manuscript of all the adverbs you can. It will be easier to spot misplaced adverbs when you can concentrate on this single problem.

I'm asking you to trust me on this: If you try to avoid splitting every infinitive (traditionally thought of as the *to* form of a verb such as *to write* or *to love*) by always putting your adverbs right after the verb instead of after the *to*, you will end up with some very awkward sentences. And here's a mind-blower: According to grammar experts, the *to* in infinitives isn't really part of the infinitive. No, you really don't need to know the intricacies here—and probably don't want to. I'm only telling you so that rather than believe what you sometimes hear about the "rules" of grammar, you'll examine questionable construction and give some weight to your own better instincts unless you aren't a native speaker of English.

The Elements of Style by William Strunk Jr., E. B. White, and Roger Angell gives examples of how improperly placed adverbs can affect meaning. I don't highly recommend *Elements* because so many writers mistake it for a book of grammar rules. It was never intended for that purpose. The content was inspired to guide Strunk's students to use his preferred *style choices* (and yes, to avoid some grammar mistakes), so it can be useful when readers don't take its every suggestion as a commandment. If you do have a copy (and love it) and your copy has been on your desk as long as mine has, consider buying an updated (fourth) edition (bit.ly/ElementsStyle) to get the latest information. Our language is always changing, but television geared up those changes and the Web reset them to warp speed. But, please. If you use it, don't accept everything it tells you as written in stone.

EDITING YOUR ADVERBS IS LIKE MINING METAPHOR GOLD

Remember the *Reader's Digest* feature "Toward More Picturesque Speech?" Over the decades, this entertaining little piece of Americana caused many writers to fall in love with metaphors. Writers who want to liven up their copy can edit adverbs so they produce those much-loved figures of speech.

When I spoke to the Small Publishers of North America (SPAN) years ago, a new writer in the audience asked if there was a list of good metaphors that he could use to improve the imagery in his writing. I told him that if there was, it would probably be a list of clichés or a list of what would fast become clichés once everyone started using them. That was before I knew this adverb trick I'm going to share with you— one that can yield metaphor gold. It works better— much better—than any list of clichés ever could.

Your search for adverbs can yield metaphors or similes because they offer associations that let you insert flecks of gold into your copy. In the "she-ran-quickly" example we used before, you determined that the adverb is redundant. *Running*, by its nature, is quick. However, you want more than *quick*. Ask, quickly as what? You might come up with a comparison where you must use the words *like* or *as* to make the image come alive. If so, you've found a simile. But if you come up with a true metaphor—where the comparison of the image is evident without the *like* or *as*—you've found something better than gold. You've found a metaphor.

Note: You can do something similar with clichés by reworking them. Before you strike something like "He was just small potatoes" from your copy, try substituting words in the offending phrase (adjectives, nouns, verbs) with something similar. One critique group I lead came up with other phrases for *small potatoes*—some were better. Some were worse. Some imparted similar meanings and some different: *Small fry; excess produce, misshapen fruit, genetically flawed apples, rejected produce, overripe avocados, bruised tomatoes.* You can see the list could get longer and longer and one of the alternatives might be something that would work well for you including adding another dimension to a character's personality—perhaps his or her unfamiliarity with English idioms.

This kind of edit can open doors for better imagery—help give your reader a visual or other sensory experience. It can also suggest possibilities for humor—something that might be welcomed by agents or publishers skimming query letters or proposals that are dull way too often.

Now, as much as I love well conceived metaphors and similes, I need to add a word of caution. I once saw an advertisement in *Writer's Digest* where a teacher (or editor) had red-penciled a note near some text that had used a metaphor. It said, "You may want to reconsider this metaphor." The reason? The metaphor was a stretch. Metaphors should be so integrated into the flow of the copy that the reader hardly notices them (unless they are intentionally used for humor). They should add to the reader's pleasure, not distract him. When a writer falls in love with her own image-making skills, she might let them undermine her first goal—that of *writing clearly*.

One of the advantages of editing adverbs—indeed any kind of systematic editing—is that you'll begin to write more concisely. The beauty of adverbs is that they can help you do that, but only if you let each one be your mentor—even if it means whacking the ones that don't work. When you do, the gremlins might spot a professional and move to greener fields.

Now let's move along to discuss some trouble-causing speech patterns that gremlins love to see you subconsciously write into your copy.

CHAPTER ELEVEN
DEATH TO GERUNDS, PARTICIPLES, AND OTHER UGLY *INGS*

Wait! I know your eyes began to look as if they were afflicted with inoperable cataracts at the very mention of the grammatical terms in the title of this chapter. Try not to yawn, though. You might need this information even if you think you already know what these monikers mean. Bear with me and I'll make it relatively painless. At the very least, you might need to be reminded why these everyday parts of speech aren't always good guys.

We can use the Find Function to help eliminate unattractive gerunds and participles. (I know you can't wait for me to refresh your memory on these terms. Be patient. It's coming!) Though not all gerunds and participles are ugly, they do tend to slow down our copy and make it wordy. They coax us to use longer, less readable sentences. They get us into dangling-participle trouble. They can even lead us to use passive constructions (which isn't always a bad thing—more on that later). Still, we want to identify them and use them only when they benefit rather than detract.

Gremlins adore all these constructions we use but were never taught to identify. They are difficult even for expert editors to detect because they are ingrained into our speech patterns. You must be prepared to eradicate them yourself.

We often hear the term *dangling participle*. It has a near-poetic ring to it. Trouble is, it is sometimes apparent that the person who uses the term doesn't know what one is. Knowing all the grammatical terms might not be an earth-trembling gap in knowledge for us writers as long as our grasp on grammar is sufficient to keep us from making errors. Still, knowing the terms helps us discuss how to avoid grammatical booboos—even ones with fancy names. So here goes.

DANGLING PARTICIPLES OFTEN COME WITH TATTLETALE *INGS*

A participle is a kind of verb, usually identified with an *ed*, an *ing,* or more rarely an *en* hanging off the end of it. They are often attached to the verb that comes after what we used to call helper verbs when we were in grade school. You know *helpers*: The *haves* and *hases* that help give verbs their tenses.

However, *dangling* participles are not called *dangling* because they come at the ends of multi-part verbs or because those endings dangle from their verbs' roots. They're called *dangling* because writers use them to modify something other than what that same writer intended. It's because they *dangle* apart from what they are supposed to modify.

Dangling participles are easier to spot if you know sentence constructions; they come in sentences with clauses. An *ing* that is attached to a verb in one or more of those clauses is a siren warning of a possible dangling-participle offense.

Example of a dangler: "Tired of reading copy with dangling modifiers, the galley went soaring across the office right into the round file."

You might sense what the author intended here, but we all know that galleys can't read copy; thus this sentence illustrates a dangling modifier. When we examine the structure, the meaning is illogical. These danglers are tricky to edit because the author knows what she is trying to say and doesn't notice the error (or the humor it creates). Sometimes readers and editors sense what the author is trying to say, too. That is why it's best to get an *experienced* editor to look at your work, even if she does have a short temper and sends galleys soaring across the room. Not to worry. You are probably paying that editor. She'll retrieve your galley and rework the offending sentence. Even though this is not a flick-of-the-pencil edit, she'll probably be tactful enough not to let you know how your danglers tried her patience. Here are two possible edits:

Edit #1: "Tired of reading copy with dangling modifiers, the editor threw the galley into the round file."

Edit #2: "The editor was so tired of reading copy with dangling modifiers, she threw her client's galley into the round file."

If she's a good editor, she'll suggest edits that retain the tone of your sentence. Because of her patience, your agent or publisher will never know you made a dangling error. That's a relief, no?

So, pay no attention to the scary grammar words and set the Find Function in your Word program to *ing*(space) or *ing*(period or comma). Use the spacebar to keep the find tool focused on *ings* at the ends of words rather than the ones hanging about in the middle of a word. From there, you can dissect your dependent clauses to see how they modify your independent clauses. Don't do it when you're tired. Do it when you know you can clobber the gremlins.

GERUND *INGS* CAN KEEP YOU FROM LAUGHING ALL THE WAY TO THE BANK

Here is another way to analyze each of the *ings* you find in your search. Let's examine one you are likely to find in your query letter. It will probably occur in a sentence like, "Writing is something I always wanted to do." *Writing* is a gerund because the magic of the English language lets us change the verb *write* into a noun by adding *ing* so it can become part of the subject phrase of that sentence. Unfortunately, it also makes the sentence wordy and not very direct. Won't "I always wanted to write" do? Or improve your sentence?

We will talk about more *ings* in a minute, but while we're on the subject of this particular use of a gerund, you can probably find something more pertinent and original to tell an agent than that you "always wanted to write." Too many writers say that to impress gatekeepers in the publishing business when they can't think of much else to tell them. Instead use the space in your one-page letter allotted to this kind of information to tell the agent that you've taken writing classes, published a poem, or spent ten years honing your marketing skills at retreats or prestigious writers' conferences to prepare for the publishing adventure ahead. Tell them you won a poetry contest in the sixth grade or that your only claim to writing fame is winning the citywide spelling bee when you were fifteen. At least that's interesting. You're trying to sell your writing (and your voice!) here. When you analyze your *ings*, you are forced to be more specific about details (including your own writing skills and experience), and that might be a big reason why you grab down an advance from Farrar, Straus and Giroux.

A PARTICIPLE *ING* IS NOT A GERUND'S TWIN

Your find utility will also pick out the *ing* in a an awful sentence like "Writing from the age of five, I became interested in telling the story of the culture I was raised in." In this sentence, *writing* is a verb that screws itself up to describe something. In this case, "Writing from the age of five" is a modifying clause that tells *when* the action happened.

Participles (words like *writing* in the example above that are formed from a verb and used as part of a modifier) often don't relate well to the rest of the sentence. In this case, the age of the writer is not that pertinent to either the meaning or the tone of the independent clause. It is an example of what happens when an author tries to pack too many bits of information into a sentence. A gatekeeper will not only notice, she'll yawn . . . or cringe.

Your sentences with participles in them might not be as bad as the example I've given, but you get the idea. A sentence like my participle example can be edited in myriad ways. Certainly, "I became interested in telling the story of the culture I was raised in," might work even though a few meticulous grammarians like Strunk and White prefer to avoid using a preposition at the end of the sentence. That is one of the reasons I take issue with Strunk. There is nothing wrong with ending a sentence with a preposition. His preferred *style choice* has only made some *think* it's bad English to do so. However, in the interest of not offending a gatekeeper who might also have been convinced about the undesirability of end-of-sentence prepositions, you might try, "Early on I became interested in . . . ." Or, if you must get that early age into the mix, "I began to write when I was five and soon became interested in fiction" will do the trick.

Try several edits to see which is more to the point, moves the sentence along better, is more dramatic at whatever it is you are trying to achieve.

Using your word processor's find function is like running a fine-toothed comb through your copy, but *you* must do the hard work. Only you can pick apart the sentences in which your *ings* occur to see if they are effective (rarely) and decide how to fix them.

WAS-*ING* AND WERE-*ING*

I recently became intimate with a Brit. When I'm on the freeway with nothing to do but drive, Michel Thomas teaches me Spanish with his series of CDs. He might been the first to coin the phrase "wuzzing and whirring" because he dislikes using scary grammar terms (one of the reasons I love that man!). In spite of the fact that I just hit you with awful words like *gerunds* and *participles*, I hate to use them, too.

In this discussion of was-*ing* and were-*ing*, I'm not going to do that. Suffice it to say that most of us use the helper verbs *was*, *were*, *have* and a few others when the *simple past* would do just fine. We also often use the future tense helper verb *will* when none is needed. That is true when writing nonfiction and narrative, but using helpers when they are unnecessary can happen anytime, anywhere. Use your Find Function to examine each one of them and see if you can eradicate a few.

Here's an example from one of my early query letters: "*This Is the Place* has won eight awards." Really? How does the word *has* clarify tense? The book won awards, plain and simple. The winning action of each award is over and done with. Why drag on a poor agent's ears with needless *hases*, *haves*, and their cousins?

My husband was required to memorize a list of helping verbs in the seventh grade. He says, "I never forgot them because my teacher grouped them together like lines in a poem so it had rhythm, some alliteration, assonance, and even rhyme." They are:

be, is, been, being,
am, are, was, were,
do, did, done, doing,
will, would,
shall, should,
can, could,
may, might, must.

I use my find tool on each word on this list. It's time consuming, but these individual searches also identify overuse of future perfect, past perfect, and other tenses that require more than one verb when simple future and past would work just as well or better. That means you chop at them as if you were tackling wordiness—which you are. It also helps identify passive constructions.

CHAPTER TWELVE
WIPE OUT YOUR INEFFECTIVE PASSIVES

Writers hear a lot about passives—mostly negative stuff. When they are overused your sentences might lead to confusion or even cause your readers to nod off. Like everything else in our speech—including expletives—there is a reason we have them (and use them). Speaking of passive construction, you should assess how you use them in everything you write.

Note: Writers often forget that *should* is a word that has psychological impact. A good chunk of the population dislikes being preached or dictated to. There are many ways to suggest that a person *should* do something without being so blatant about it. Even how-to books where readers expect to be told what they *should* do should use the word as rarely as possible. The last sentence in the paragraph above illustrates how the word *should* can impart an unintended (or intended) tone of authoritarianism.

In passive sentences, a noun (generally a deceptive or false noun) comes first, the verb second, but the actual doer-of-the-verb (the subject that is being downgraded) comes last or becomes invisible. Though the words *there is* or *there are* and helping verbs are often part of the equation (see "was-*ing* and were-*ing*" in Chapter Eleven), passive doesn't always tip its hand to the reader or listener so easily. To turn passive constructions into active ones, see the next sidebar.

So what is good about passives? They allow the writer to avoid providing the real subject of the verb up front where it belongs in an active sentence. You may not agree that this quirk of the English language that lets reporters and interviewers deflect blame for questions that might otherwise be interpreted as rude can ever be a good thing. It may be unattractive, but it's useful.

We hear, "It has been suggested that you were instrumental in the coup." Because passive construction is hard to identify, it is all the more useful for obfuscation. Politicians might say, "It was determined by the committee that the problem couldn't be avoided." If I were writing about a corrupt politician, I'd let him use passive constructions in a whole lot of his dialogue. Servers who hope to receive a sizable tip might apologize by saying, "I'm sorry that the steak was not cooked to your satisfaction." The cook who braised the steak isn't mentioned. It is as if the great-chef-in-the-sky let the clouds part to present you with something so precious that any criticism would be sacrilegious. The server didn't mess up or if he did, he didn't own up. There are other grammatical things going on here, but you get the idea.

So what is the official definition of passive? June Casagrande, my plain-speaking grammarian friend, says, ". . . passive voice occurs when the object of a transitive verb is made the grammatical subject of a sentence." To her credit she does this *after* she's explained passives without using that scary word *transitive*. It is fun (and even necessary) to get a solid (albeit technical) explanation. She thinks so and I think so, if only because there is so much misunderstanding surrounding the passive voice.

Volumes have been written on the subject of passive construction and they're often misleading or downright wrong—especially on the Web. Here are two trustworthy resources:

- Rutgers University gives examples of how politicos and others use passive to weasel out of stuff; you'll find them amusing and edifying: andromeda.rutgers.edu/~jlynch/Writing/p.html.
- Purdue offers more on passives at owl.english.purdue.edu/owl/resource/601/02/ and owl.english.purdue.edu/owl/resource/601/02/.

Passive construction can be used by writers to manipulate tone, voice, and intent. Consider using it if you are writing copy for TV ads for pharmaceutical companies, dialogue for a wimp or a passive aggressive personality, if you are intentionally slowing the pace of your work (say you want to place your story in an earlier time when language and life were less hurried), or if you want to portray a b-o-o-oring personality. The teacher in the movie classic *Ferris Buehler's Day Off* comes to mind.

The information box on the next page helps you more easily identify passive constructions.

SIDEBAR
Easy Test to Keep Passives
from Inducing a Snooze

Ask yourself if what appears to be the subject of the sentence is doing anything or is it having something done to it. Here are some passive sentences.

- "The book was written by Barbara" is a passive sentence. *The book* is idle. Barbara is doing the action, but she isn't the subject of the sentence.
- "The book was written." This is a passive sentence with no indication of what the true subject is. You can see that this passive sentence leaves Barbara out of the grammatical equation.
- "Barbara wrote the book." This is an active sentence. It is also an example of how passive sentences can be edited. If "by Barbara" is never mentioned, you might have to do some research or substitute something for the information that has been so cleverly omitted.

A little box at the bottom of the Readability Statistics feature in Word gives you your Passive Sentence scores. (Learn more in Chapter Nine.) You can also search on phrases like *there is*, *there are*, the preposition *by*, and the helping verbs listed in Chapter Eleven. When you are done with your search, check your Readability Statistic score. If it still looks too high, enlist the eyes of someone who knows their English grammar, especially someone who hates the all too frequently used passive voice.

##

At the risk of being repetitive, please note that we wouldn't have ugly *ings*, passive constructions, and anything else I disparage in the English language if they weren't useful, but you want to be sure you are using them in ways that contribute to clear and concise writing, writing that moves the way you want it to.

I often tell my students that they should have a very good reason for keeping ugly stuff, a reason that can be verbalized. "I just like it that way" usually isn't sufficient. I sometimes use passive voice in this book. Here's my "very good reason" for using them when I discuss grammar: They let me avoid using complicated grammatical terms as the subjects of my sentences.

Now you have mastered the passive voice—how to avoid it and how to use it when it's needed. I mean, what would pharmaceutical companies do if it didn't exist? If you don't believe me, your homework is to listen carefully to the voiceovers on the TV ads for Premarin or Humera these days. They're hard to listen to and obviously disguising what they don't want you to know but are required by law to reveal.

Mmm. That' uncomfortable to think about, so let's move on to something more fun—supercharging your dialogue.

CHAPTER THIRTEEN
GETTING RID OF DIALOGUE MIGRAINES

Warning here! If you write nonfiction exclusively, don't skip this section. Reporters for the world's most-respected newspapers have always quoted those they interview and taken quotations from their sources, but journalists writing straight news realize the value of anecdotes now more than ever before. The most accomplished journalists may now discard who, how, what, and where leads in favor of memorable anecdotes—even anecdotes with dialogue.

The danger with using dialogue in your writing is that, unless you—the writer of fiction or nonfiction— have read a lot of fiction and have a knack for absorbing the nuances of what you see on a page, you might get dialogue wrong.

Miserably wrong.

Your reader might not be able to pinpoint what went awry, but she'll know something is amiss because since she learned to read she has been trained to expect certain dialogue indicators and forms. When writers wing it, their readers sense it.

Even when writers have a good reason for deviating from guidelines, the reader will be distracted by the departure in style. When I first opened the famous memoir *Angela's Ashes* (bit.ly/AngelasAsh), I was uncomfortable with the lack of conventional quotation marks around author Frank McCourt's dialogue and didn't realize what was bothering me for a while. In fact, I was so distracted I had trouble getting into the story.

McCourt had a very good reason for choosing not to use traditional quotation marks. He had manufactured his dialogue. By that I mean he couldn't remember *everything* that had been said exactly as it was said when he was four and memoirs are supposed to be factual. Avoiding quotation marks was his way of being honest. Still, the quotes in dialogue are *understood* to be a convention and people (even gatekeepers) forgive using them in both memoirs and in fiction where dialogue is obviously imaginary. I think McCourt made a mistake, but I also give him credit for making a style choice he thought was conducive to his kind of storytelling. If you want to review McCourt's dialogue, you can read a few pages—free—on Amazon using their Look Inside feature for that book.

Note: If you want the full story on writing great dialogue, read Writer's Digest book titled *Writing Dialogue* (bit.ly/Chiarella) by Tom Chiarella. What I give you here will polish the editing aspects of your dialogue, but if it needs extensive revision, well, Chiarella has written a whole book on it.

Tip: You can strengthen your characters' personalities with the way they talk as you edit. Leora Krygier imagined a character for her novel

Finding Maynard. Maynard uses the word *except* as an indication of an indecisive personality. Krygier uses Word's find function to trace the *excepts* in that character's dialogue. She checked to make sure she used the word enough to help the reader subconsciously identify this speech pattern with the character but not so that the technique became noticeable or annoying to the reader. You can use repetitive physical mannerisms in the same way. In my novel *This Land Divided*, Gram Harriet sniffs when she makes a demand that she expects to be obeyed.

AMATEUR DIALOGUE TAGS CAN BE BIG HEADACHES

Dialogue is often an agent's or editor's first indication that a submission is written by someone with little or no training in the craft of writing. Because your dialogue tags—those silly little *he said/she said* things that help readers keep track of who said what—are a big part of your editing if you didn't do it in your revision. Fixing them often entails doing more than removing them when they are unnecessary or by changing a word or two. You might as well take a double look at them while you are in your editing mode.

Of course, there's a lot more to editing dialogue than reconsidering the tags. Here are ten easy ways to improve your dialogue without reading whole books or taking a seminar on the subject, though you would probably learn something new (even after reading this book!) or be inspired anew if you did.

- Keep it simple. *He said* or *she said* will usually do. Your reader has been trained to accept this repetition.
- Forget you ever heard of strong verbs (just for the purpose of editing dialogue—then go back to your strong verb mode). Skip the *he yelped* and the *she sighed*. They slow your dialogue. If you feel you need them, look at the words—the actual dialogue—your character used when he was yelping. Maybe it doesn't reflect the way someone would sound if he yelped. Maybe if you strengthen the dialogue, you could ditch the overblown tag without losing any meaning.
- When you can, reveal who is saying something by the voice or tone of the dialogue. That way you might be able to skip tags occasionally, especially when you have only two people speaking to one another. Your dialogue will ring truer, too.
- Having characters use other characters' names to identify who is speaking is the lazy writer's attempt at clarity. In real life, we tend to reserve using names for times when we are angry, disapproving, or we just met in a room full of people and we're practicing our social skills. Overuse of names in dialogue might annoy a reader enough to distract her from your story.
- Avoid putting *internal* dialogue in italics *or* in quotation marks. When you write in a character's point of view, your readers know who is thinking the words. Point of view is a convention of literature and writers need to

learn how to make it work for them instead of taking the easy way out.

- Be cautious about using dialogue to tell something that should be narrated or described. It does not help to transfer the telling or exposition from the narrator to the dialogue. It does make the character who is speaking sound longwinded and negate one of the things dialogue does well—that is, move the pace of the story forward quickly. Putting quotation marks around exposition is the lazy writer's approach to revision.

- Don't break up dialogue sequences with long or overly frequent blocks of narrative. That, too, keeps dialogue from moving the story along. If a writer inserts too much stage direction or pet descriptions, it loses its forward motion along with the tension it is building.

- Avoid having every character answer a question directly. Some people do that (perhaps a sensitive young girl who has been reared to obey her elders), but many don't. Some veer off with an answer that doesn't follow from the question asked. Some are silent. Some characters do any one of these things as a matter of course. Some do them purposefully, maybe to avoid fibbing or to change the subject or because they are passive aggressive.

- Avoid dull dialogue that doesn't help draw better characters or move the action forward. Forcing a reader to hear people introduce themselves to one another without a very good reason to do so is cruel and unusual punishment.

- Use dialogue to plant a seed of intrigue unobtrusively. When a character brings up a concern that is not solved immediately, the page-turning effect of your story is heightened. Just don't forget to answer the question raised at another appropriate time in your story.

DIALOGUE PUNCTUATION HEADACHES

I won't tell you that punctuating dialogue is easy. It is an intricate process and is made more so because the edition of *Mother Goose's Nursery Rhymes* and other classics you were raised on probably used British punctuation rules and caused you to alternate between American and British punctuation guidelines ever since. In addition, the Internet, stylebooks, and some popular experimental writers have begun to influence punctuation rules.

The thing is, an agent or acquisition editor will not care whether you chose to depart from generally accepted guidelines for punctuating dialogue, made errors out of ignorance, or a gremlin attacked your copy. She or he might simply judge your submission amateurish. It is acceptance you are after, not winning a quibble over dialogue etiquette. Later—when you are famous (and respected), you might be able to do some influencing of your own. In the meantime, unless you are from the UK, use American protocol and be glad that we made it simpler than the Brits did. More on that later.

I worry when one of my editing clients becomes adamant over a matter of opinion or taste, especially when she or he deserves a key to the door to success. It is best to know the rules for dialogue, abide by them, and change them (if you must) only after your work has been accepted or once you are known and don't have to get by an arbiter. See the information box below for some essential guidelines.

SIDEBAR
Making Dialogue Punctuation Easy

Here are a few guidelines for using punctuation that won't chill an editor's ardor.

- Introduce dialogue after a standard dialogue tag (the *he said/she said* kind) with a comma.
  Example: John said, "Please help me with my dialogue."

- Use a colon to introduce a quotation after an independent clause.
  Example: This is what John says we should do to edit dialogue tags: "Go very slowly. Check them one-by-one."

  - Capitalize the first letter within the quotation as if the sentence began there even if what is said is a fragment. That's how people talk. It doesn't change dialogue punctuation.

  - **Example**: John said, "Don't go there." He paused. "Because you won't like what you see."

Here is where—too often—we get confused:

- A period ends a sentence and *always* goes *inside* the quotation marks that come after the quoted sentence.
  Example: John said, "If anything comes up that is not covered by these few guidelines, even a good editor might have to research ways to punctuate around quotation marks."

Cont'd

- Commas, too, go *inside* the quotation marks. Even when the quotation marks *don't* come at the end of a sentence. **Example**: "Even a good editor," John said, "might have to research some arcane grammar rules." (The second comma in the sentence is governed by the first rule in this sidebar on page 137.)

- Exclamation points, question marks, semicolons, and even dashes go within the quotation marks *when they apply to the quotation itself.* Put them *outside* the quotation marks when they apply to the whole sentence. **Example One**: John shook his fist. "I hate it that way!" **Example Two**: "I don't care what you think about Jane's calmly saying, 'I don't care for that'!" See how the exclamation point comes outside of the quotation marks that indicate what Jane says calmly? In this example, it is the speaker who is vehement, not Jane, who happens to be calm.

- Colons, by default, go *outside* quotation marks, and if I do say so, look as if gremlins have been at work, probably because the rule is so frequently ignored. Trust me. Even if you think a colon should be inside the curly guys, put it outside.
- If you need to use parentheses at the end of the sentence and after a quotation, the period goes after the parenthetical expression. Use something like this example from a book proposal: **Example**: N. B. Harrow says, "Memoirs about drug addiction are on the upswing since Frey's fiasco" (see www.xxx.com for the original source). No period after *fiasco*. Put the period *after* the closed parentheses.

##

Use Word's Find Function to check your dialogue tags and your punctuation. In each case, consider the rules in the sidebar box above. You can use this same check to see if you have overworked your dialogue tags. Don't use tags when voice and other cues will do the job. Punctuation considerations more intricate than these can usually be avoided by rearranging the structure of your sentences. By doing so, you will circumvent the rare occasion when you don't follow the rules perfectly or when an agent thinks she knows correct usage but doesn't and (yikes!) judges your correct choice as incorrect.

In *On Writing* (bit.ly/KingsOnWriting), Stephen King tells us that a dialogue tag can dictate the use of punctuation in the dialogue itself. For instance, if the tag uses a form of the word *ask*, avoid using a question mark at the end of what the character said. That makes sense. We try to avoid being redundant. Here are examples of ways to avoid punctuation redundancy:

- He asked, "How old are you." (Note the period after the question when the dialogue is tagged with *asked.*)
- He said, "How old are you?" (Note the tag uses the word *said*, not *asked.*)
- "How old are you?" (No tags at all.)

It might seem like a small thing, but an agent or editor might give you extra points for observing King's suggestion.

OK. So much for thwarting the dialogue gremlins. Let's see how the ubiquitous media negatively influences our writing and opens the door for gremlins to make grand entrances.

SECTION FIVE

CANDY AND VEGGIES FOUND IN THE MEDIA

CHAPTER FOURTEEN
VIRUSES AREN'T THE ONLY COMMUNICABLE DISEASE CONTRACTED FROM THE NET

The Net is a miracle worker. It is also a tool gremlins have coopted to lure unsuspecting authors into using tried-and-true tools in new and sometimes disconcerting ways. The Internet is new. The publishing world is . . . well . . . both old and traditional. What might work well in an e-mail (smiling faces, anyone?) will not impress in the world of publishing. That includes the world of self-publishing because books published independently must pass even more intense scrutiny from librarians, bookstore buyers, contest judges, and readers so steeped in tradition from past reading that anything new or cutsie diverts their concentration from content to unrelated questions—or criticism.

There is another problem with the Net. Webmasters, bloggers, and e-zine editors must work quickly. The Internet and the ease of publishing white papers and e-books fast might lead us astray. Some so-called writers even use programs that help them write whole automated books, much of the text "borrowed" from the copy (and brains) of someone else.

What we see in the publishing world these days is often carelessly written. We see some errors so frequently we come to believe they are not mistakes nor recognize they are affectations. We see them so often we pay no attention to them. Worse. We emulate them either because they seem useful or fresh or (gasp!) we think they're cute.

Doing that might not be the worst thing for a casual blogger, but if we are professionals, if we want a career using our computers, brains, and pens, we must take responsibility for what soaks into our craft via our subconscious. If you don't think that can happen, consider how we are told that when we read great literature, some of the technique will seep in, just as we instinctively knew bad grammar from good long before we heard a teacher expound on subjects and verbs.

This responsibility thing is lots of work because, though language has always changed, it changes more quickly now than ever before. To assume that because we once learned something one way, it will always be accepted is fallacious thinking. To neglect researching the language we write in when we so assiduously research the facts for what we write is folly. I talk about some of the communicable diseases many of us can contract next. Let's immunize ourselves.

GETTING CUTE WITH CAPS

Words typed in all caps are used on the Web more and more.

- Authors want to make the titles of their books stand head and shoulders above the copy in any given piece. One can hardly blame them, but using italics is more dignified and preferred.
- Some use them to show that a word should be emphasized when professionals have a

perfectly-acceptable way to do that. It is called italics.

- Some big publishers are setting the first few words of a chapter in all-caps as a design choice that helps alert readers to a new chapter. All-cap headlines help forewarn readers that they are encountering something new— especially in digital forms.
- Some book designers think all-caps headers look nice.
- Some writers use all-caps to indicate that the writer is yelling.

Stop! Reserve your use of all-caps for places where they work. Don't use them where they say something you don't want them to say or are substitutes for time-honored practices. Readers don't like to be yelled at even when they sympathize with the idea of making one's title stand out. Avoid using them in any manuscript or document used to sell a manuscript. If a publisher wants to use them in your book's *design*, that is a different story. If a publisher wants to use them as part of the *text*, I might tactfully suggest they reconsider. The good news is all-caps can be spotted easily during your first manual edit.

Note: You might have noticed that I use all-cap subtitles in the chapters of this book. I can back that choice up with three good reasons. 1. All-caps alert a reader—especially those who are reading on a screen—to the beginning of a new topic or section. 2. All-caps used in this way allow a book designer or formatter to delineate new sections without changing typefaces (fonts) which can also be overdone. 3. Some font choices are not supported by the underlying mechanisms of digital printing and this book is also available as an e-book. Other choices like boldface and italics have their own sets of drawbacks. I know, decisions, decisions.

EFFUSIVE ITALICS

Many books are self- and subsidy-published these days and many are put together by marginally qualified editors (or no editor at all!). It has become common practice to italicize a character's internal dialogue. In fact, this affectation has become so widespread you occasionally find italics used this way in fiction published by the best and brightest of the New York publishing houses.

Even with the hallowed examples of these few publishers tempting you, don't use italics this way. Most acquisition editors realize that writers—even experienced writers—use italics as a crutch for avoiding the techniques they have not yet mastered (or are unaware they exist). It's more important that you grow as a writer rather than take the easy way.

In *Wired for Story* published by Ten Speed Press (bit.ly/WiredStory), Lisa Cron says, ". . . I'd venture to say you have probably read hundreds of books written in the third person that clued you into what the characters were thinking so deftly that when it comes to figuring out exactly how they did it, you are still wondering whether you should italicize or put quotation marks around sentences that must then be clearly tagged as thoughts. The answer is, none of the above. No italics. No quotation marks. No tags." (We talked about tags and quotation marks in the dialogue section of Chapter Thirteen.)

Lisa *does* note that one author uses italics for telepathic speech effectively. That reminds us that authors are arbiters of their style choices. Nevertheless, one fine author lost a highly desirable publisher because he wouldn't budge on the question of italics in his own book. Authors need to know what may be at stake when they don't make gatekeeper-friendly choices.

Dr. Bob Rich prefers to use a left margin indent to distinguish a speech, dream, contents of a letter or other long tracts of speech instead of italics.

Lisa's "none of the above" advice applies to stories told in first person or from other points of view. There is no need to use italics for internal thought when there are time-honored techniques that don't take your reader out of the story when they see little squiggly letters where they aren't needed. You will be writing from a specific point of view and your reader will be aware of what that POV is if you've done it well.

When you are writing in a particular point of view you are choosing to let your character do the work instead of inserting yourself or another narrator. You can usually get away without using tags like *she wondered* and *he thought*, and you should when you don't *need* them for clarity. When possible, use tags that are less distinguishable as tags. They might show how a character is moving or what he sees in his surroundings (which may reflect how he is feeling), and you can do that without anything that resembles, "He looked around and noticed . . . ." When you're in his point of view, everything—*everything*—that is being observed is being observed by him. Just be sure to use body language tags and observation tags to tell the reader something she doesn't already know from the context of the story.

We know you want to develop your craft or you wouldn't be reading this book. So develop your technique by reading books like Lisa's and by paying attention to the techniques great authors use when you read. As Lisa says, it's hard to do because their skill goes unnoticed. Italics do *not* go unnoticed. If that were OK, why would excellent writers like Elizabeth George go to pains to write without using them? Writers must trust their own skills as writers and trust their readers' ability to read well. Most readers have been reading a long time and subconsciously know those anti-italics techniques, too. Typography is not part of this equation. Careful editing and writing are.

Using italics for internal dialogue in a document that introduces your craft to those who accept or reject your work will indicate to them that you are not an experienced writer. Those first three chapters you will probably be asked to submit are important. Don't give your reader something to criticize unnecessarily. If your manuscript is accepted in spite of this affectation and you are assigned a good editor, you will probably be expected to edit all those italics out before press time.

After you become familiar with the find function for editing (read more about this in Section Three of this book) you will see why corrections of this type are more quickly made during your first manual edit, or better still, in the revision process before you ever get to the editing stage.

Even italics used correctly for emphasis can be a distraction if used too extensively. Once a copy was submitted to me that made me think the author believed 90% of her manuscript was emphasis-worthy.

QUOTATION MARKS FOR THE TOO-DUMB READER?

Using quotation marks for emphasis or because we think our readers need to be told what to think about words they have known since childhood is epidemic. We use them inappropriately for emphasis. For colloquialisms. For slang. For humor. Because we are in love with them. Therefore, I plead with you not to skip this section. Plead! For you it might be just a review, but if it turns out you need information on using quotation marks worse than you thought, you can e-mail me later to thank me for getting down on my knees to you.

When I attended a master class provided for UCLA Extension Writers' Program instructors, one of our most popular teachers bemoaned the use of quotation marks around words that are merely slang and not irony or sarcasm. Using quotation marks for irony or sarcasm indicates the words are not what they seem. He said that using them to designate slang is a mark of an amateur because readers *know* what slang means unless they are ESL students, in which case they will need more than a couple of curlicues to get the meaning. He suggested that when a writer's work is intended for an English-speaking audience, they will understand your meaning without the quotation marks. He said we should "just ditch them."

Notice I did not put quotation marks around the word *ditch*? By avoiding them, I acknowledge that you—as a speaker and writer of English—know that the colloquial interpretation of *ditch* is *get rid of.* If not, I know you could guess from context. You do not need to be instructed on that point. It is a bit insulting to suppose you would. We do not use quotation marks to teach people what they already know.

I apologize for not crediting the instructor who pointed out this inappropriate use of italics, but I have "forgotten" who it was. Yes, with those quotation marks around *forgotten*, I am showing that I really haven't forgotten at all, that I'm actually indicating that I remember him well. There is even a subtle suggestion that I am a little miffed with him for exploding a favorite writers' affectation and you can surmise that my tone might be tinged with sarcasm. So, now you've got it. Use quotation marks for:

- Irony.
- Sarcasm
- To set off dialogue (and we limit that to dialogue we presume is or was spoken *aloud*).
- Sometimes for titles. The Index in this book lets you find more information on titles and exactly which titles call for italics and which call for quotation marks.

Note: Even though some of the edits in this section might be made more accurately on your hardcopy, your computer's find tool can be an effective weapon against them. It will easily find quotation marks in your text; it is up to you whether you want to edit them manually, use your program's find function, or use a combination of both.

- Do not use quotation marks around words not actually being spoken by a character, even if he is silently saying these words to himself.
- That quotation marks appear around a word or phrase on a sign somewhere does not give one *carte blanche* to emulate the sign maker's ignorance. A sign—however permanent—does not mean the grammar is impeccable. Here is an example: **Brake Inspections Done "Free."** Now, what are we supposed to make of that? Are they free or are they not? (See the sidebar "Titles Are Tattletales" in Chapter Five for more on quotation marks.)
- Do not use quotation marks around any word like colloquialisms or slang that native speakers will understand without them.
- Do not use quotation marks around numbers or letters for which the symbols rather than the written words are used. Like CD or TV or like *p* and *q*.
- Use italics rather than quotation marks to indicate a word stands for itself.
  Example: "The word *ditch* can be used colloquially to mean *avoid*."

  Example: Do *not* use: "The word 'ditch' can be used colloquially to mean 'avoid.'" You can see how it might even result in having to use double quotation marks unnecessarily.

##

151

Check Chapter Thirteen for getting rid of other dialogue migraines, the sidebar "Making Dialogue Punctuation Easy," and the Index in this book for other quotation mark transgressions. They are trouble causers in a variety of situations.

QUESTION MARKS AND EXCLAMATION POINTS RUNNING AMOK

Question marks and exclamation points are fun in e-mails. With them, we can make a point without taking pains to make our writing concise. You want to avoid using multiples of either of these punctuation marks in anything other than your most casual note.

These two punctuation marks can seem overused even when we haven't used a heavy hand on their keys. How can that be? When we have done our work as writers and when our words impart the intended emotions on their own, anything more than a simple period may be redundant. Exclamation points are for commands! Or for yelling! Or for extreme excitement! But if you suggest those emotions with the words rather than the punctuation, so much the better.

What about rhetorical questions where no answer is expected? Use a period instead of a question mark. The intent of "Am I going insane?" changes dramatically when we use a period.

You can see we are working at letting craft carry the heavy load of writing expressively, rather than relying on tricks or even punctuation.

ELLIPSIS DOTS GONE WILD

Strictly speaking, an ellipsis is three periods—no fewer, no more—that take the place of something deleted from copy or something unknown or never spoken. An ellipsis is like a word or phrase's ghost. Occasionally we see four dots, but the last one is a period that would naturally occur if the end of a sentence weren't ellipted.

You might find what appears to be ellipses anywhere on the Web. As page design elements. To lead a reader from header to the body of copy. These can all be useful for writers who are doing their own formatting, setting up a Web site, or designing their own promotional fliers. However, the ones we are most concerned with as editors are the ones writers use to indicate natural pauses in dialogue or the ones used to indicate that a section of a quotation has been removed to accommodate space limitations or to aid understanding. We often use them that way to shorten quotes or to make blurbs (endorsements for our books) shorter and more readable.

I recommend a Writer's Digest book titled *Writing Dialogue* by Tom Chiarella (bit.ly/Chiarella) for fiction writers. He talks about how to write more effective dialogue using ellipses. People do occasionally trail off to silence when they speak. They pause. They slow their speech and then speed up. People also interrupt themselves and others and ellipses are sometimes used for that, too, though Chiarella prefers a dash to suggest an interruption of a sentence.

Check to be sure you have used ellipses for one of the purposes described above. You also want to see if you overused them or if their use obscures your meaning. After all, ellipses don't really say anything. An instructor at the Association of Mormon Letters Writers' Conference I spoke at noted that there is little room for ellipses in poetry (where language should be condensed). Use them only when, as an example, the absence of language says more than the language itself would say or when you are purging words unneeded for your purpose.

To analyze your ellipses, use your find tool once to edit and then again to fix the formatting which—honestly—almost no one gets right unless they are typesetters or editors at *The New Yorker*. If you did type them correctly, take yourself out for a jamoca almond fudge ice cream sundae. If you didn't, check the next information box. I mean, what if you get a publisher who doesn't know the ellipsis-formatting secret.

SIDEBAR
Making Your Ellipses Pretty

To fix ellipses, use your **Find Function**. Type two periods into the **Find What** box. It will find both those periods *and* ellipses that suffer from sticky key syndrome. Make your corrections.

Treat each dot (period) in an ellipsis as if it were a separate word. That is, tap the spacebar on either side of each one: (space)dot(space)dot(space)dot(space).

Find more on formatting ellipses in Chapter Sixteen under "Check Up on Your Formatter" where I show you how to double check the work of your formatter—the one hired by your publisher or the one you hire if you are self-publishing. It will also help you do a darn good job of formatting if you choose to self-publish and decide not to hire a formatter.

##

PRETTY-IS-AS-PRETTY-DOES AMPERSANDS

The ampersand (&) is a pretty little dude but it isn't a letter or even a word. It's a logogram that represents a word. Its history goes back to classical antiquity, but interesting history and being cute are no reason to overuse it in the interest of trying to separate your writing from the pack. It's better to concentrate on techniques that make a difference rather than gimmicks that distract. Here are legitimate uses for the ampersand.

- The Writers Guild of America uses the ampersand to indicate a closer collaboration or partnership than the word *and* suggests. It is a convenient way to subtly indicate that one writer has *not* been brought in to rewrite or fix the work of another but that they share credit equally.
- Newspapers, journals, and others choose to use ampersands when they cite sources. That's their style choice, not a grammar rule.
- Academia asks that the word *and* be spelled out in all citations.
- Occasionally the term *etc.* is abbreviated to *&c*, though I can see no reason for confusing a reader with this. *Etc.* is already an abbreviation of *et cetera* and the ampersand version saves but one letter and isn't commonly recognized.
- Ampersands are sometimes used instead of *and* to distinguish that the *and* is part of a name: "The Law Offices of Johnson & Johnson." It's also used rather than *and* when naming a complicated series of items. Wikipedia gives this example: "Rock, pop, rhythm & blues and hip hop." Even though this latter usage has been given a green light, it seems

like a stretch and an unnecessary affectation when we could but use the traditional serial comma like this: "Rock, pop, rhythm and blues, and hip hop." I would exercise my style choice rights rather than distract my reader.

For a little style guide from the point of view of academia, go to owl.english.purdue.edu/owl/resource/560/03/. To see a graphic artist's creative use of the ampersand just because it's visually attractive, go to amperart.com/subscribe/ for Chaz DeSimone's free offer. He's the cover designer of this book.

SIMPLIFY POSSESSIVES SO THE GREMLIN CAN'T MESS WITH YOU

The Internet is sometimes called the World Wide Web (www) for a very good reason. Everyone uses it. School children. Seniors. Parisians. So why would you want to take a cue on using possessives from what you see there when they seem to be a huge problem for Web designers, menu printers, and sign makers everywhere. I recently took a snapshot of one of those signs. I couldn't resist including it in this chapter, so keep reading.

Really. It is not that the possessive-plural concept is so hard to understand. It's that too often grade school teachers pass along incorrect information they were taught when they were in the fifth grade. (Once ingrained, the mistakes never seem to disappear.) It's that the United States is a nation of immigrants and they are concentrating on learning enough English to pass their citizenship tests. It's because immigrants tend to open small businesses like crazy (bless their hearts). Small businesses need signs and business owners don't want to hire someone to do something they can do themselves. Or when they do, they hire a sign maker who speaks their own first language. They forget that verbal expertise does not necessarily go hand in hand with the tricky application of decals or the art of molding letters into fluorescent shapes.

Here is what possessives are. They are words that denote *ownership* by adding an apostrophe and an *s*. Anne's dog. Archie's computer. Men's toys. A kid's bicycle.

Here is what possessives are *not*: They are not plurals denoting more than one of something. They are not Avocado's Sold Here. *Avocados* is first-choice plural in my dictionary and in this case they do not own anything other than maybe their own skin and their own pits—but that's not the intent here.

Of course, certain plurals can own something. That is the case with *Men's toys* and *Kids' bicycles*. Notice the plural word stayed the same. We only added the possessive apostrophe.

Purdue University's Web site has an online writers' lab that can be trusted. It gives a simple rule for identifying possessives, one many of us know but tend to forget. They suggest that we, "turn the suspected phrase around and make it an 'of the . . . phrase.'"

> **Example**: "The gremlin's nasty habit" can be turned into "the nasty habit *of* the gremlin," so we know for sure it is a possessive and needs the apostrophe.

Be careful not to let Purdue's *of the* technique become a habit. Use passive constructions only when you have a good reason to do so. Purdue's example is just a test. Testing . . . Testing . . . .

Find Purdue's site at owl.english.purdue.edu/. In the meantime, all the rules you need for possessives are in the sidebar "Making a Noun Own Something" on the next two pages.

I have a new iPhone so I couldn't resist taking this picture of a sign that used the possessive apostrophe incorrectly. I may have started something. It may be the beginning for a new booklet of awful signs I see when I travel. The saddest part of this one is that it isn't in a small business or a small town or even a foreign country. It's in the Amtrak Station in Savannah, Georgia, in the good old U. S. of A. Yes, it nearly made me cry. I'm still trying to figure out what these taxis *own*.

To make a noun own something:

- Add *'s* to a singular form of the word, even if it ends in *s*. Example: *Travis's uniform*. Yes, the stylebooks do disagree on this and there are what I call seat-of-the-pants exceptions. Determiners seem to be how a word sounds to you or a journal's style guidelines. If you should ever, ever, have an occasion to say, "Those white eggs's yolks are the same color as those brown eggs's yolks," I suspect you will hear how odd that sounds and make a style choice to "Those white eggs' yolks are the same color as those brown eggs' yolks." You can always make the style choice to make your plural nouns possessives with a single apostrophe and no one would come along and slap your hands. The very formal example (*Travis's uniform*) is slowly being simplified and discarded for *Travis' uniform*.

  Note: The reason *eggs's* doesn't sound right is rooted in linguistics. The two *z* sounds together annoy the ears of English speakers and jumble our tongues so we adjust our speech to our comfort level. This kind of adjustment happens in many languages if not all, and most of us don't question it. We just go with the flow.

- Add *'s* to plural words that do not end in *s*. Example: *children's*.
- Add only the apostrophe (no *s*) to the end of plural nouns that have become possessives and end in *s* like these: *(Several) eggs' yolks* and *writers' program* (because these programs are designed for more than one writer).

Cont'd

SIDEBAR
Cont'd: Making a Noun Own Something

- Add *'s* only to the last syllable of hyphenated words.
  Example: Sister-in-law's children.

- Add *'s* only to the last noun in a series to show joint possession of a single object.
  Example: Nancy and Ted's house.

- Rarely two people will possess two items; in that case, each of the owners gets a separate little marker for a possessive.
  Example: Nancy's and Ted's iPhones.

- Do not add an apostrophe to a possessive pronoun. Words of ownership like *yours*, *theirs*, and *his*, indicate possession without doing anything to them. In these cases, the gremlin usually coaxes you into an error only when you have a prepositional phrase trying to obscure the issue.
  Example: He is an enemy of *yours* (not an enemy of *yours'* or *your's*).

  Note: These rules might be slightly different—especially the rules for plural possessives—from the ones you learned in school. The updated ones are more flexible and easier. Rejoice!

  ##

OTHER FRIGHTENING APOSTROPHES

We use apostrophes to form possessives, but we also use them to form the *plurals* of some lowercase letters and to indicate the omission of letters. If you want to foil the fifteen-fingered guys, you need to know the rules and carefully examine each use during the editing process. Your computer's find tool will serve up every single apostrophe for your inspection.

So now we have mastered possessives from the section above, how do we tell the difference between them and the ones that look just like them but that we use for omissions and for making singular lower case letters into plurals.

> **Try this**: Do *not* think of the apostrophes used for omissions or for making lower case letters into plural as any relation to the apostrophes used to possessives. Think of them as their own little entities with no DNA resemblance to possessives at all. For more help, see the next information boxes on "Sneaky Uses of Apostrophes."

SIDEBAR
Sneaky Uses of Apostrophes

It would be nice if apostrophes were delegated "Use for Possessives Only." Unfortunately, languages are not designed. They grow. We are stuck with the need to know how to use apostrophes in lots of other situations, too. Here they are:

- Use apostrophes to form *plurals* of lowercase letters. We all know the rule to "Mind our p's and q's."

Cont'd

SIDEBAR
Cont'd: Sneaky Uses of Apostrophes

- Do not use apostrophes to form plurals of capital letters, numbers, or symbols. This is a new, simplified grammar rule, so you'll see examples of apostrophes used the old-fashioned way in older books or formal or academic papers. Today your editors prefer plurals like these: ATMs, Zs, 3s, and &s. You know, those that are made by adding an *s*, no less, no more.
- Use apostrophes to indicate an omission of letters. Everyone knows we use them for contractions like *can't* and *won't*. The apostrophe takes the place of the *o* and *n* we eliminated from *not*.

Note: English as second language students are often taught that contractions are not "good English." This is patently false. English without contractions feels stilted to native speakers. Ideas like this might get started in the psychological yearning for a language that is more like code than a living, breathing entity. Maybe it comes from a disdain for anything that seems too casual. Maybe students transfer information in style guides for formal academic papers to their other writing.

- Use apostrophes when you drop letters to indicate casual enunciation or dialect. Instead of *them,* we might choose *'em.* Note that your word processor may get the direction of that apostrophe backwards, so you may need to copy and paste to get it to curl toward the omitted letters.

Cont'd

SIDEBAR
Cont'd: Sneaky Uses of Apostrophes

Warning: *Till* is a word. It is *not* a contraction of *until*. Do not reason that it is a shortened version of *until* that would require an apostrophe. Reason doesn't count here.

Another caution: *Could've* (a contraction of *could have*) or *could have* is correct, not *could of*.

- Use special care with *its* and *it's*. *Its—without* the apostrophe—is the *possessive* form (just to be confusing, of course!). *It's—with* the apostrophe—is the contraction of *it is*. Ditto with *your* and *you're*. *Your* is the possessive. To test them, tease out the separate words, *it is* and *you are*. When you can make them into two words (and they make sense), then and only then can you be sure that a letter has been omitted and gets replaced with an apostrophe.

If you sometimes forget to use apostrophes where they are required, it is probably better to rely on the old manual editing approach. For that, go through your copy and check every word. You *could* use your computer's find tool to search on all words that end in *s* by keying s(space) in the find box, but I think using your computer is just as time-consuming as a manual edit (and thus very *un*frugal!) because you might find other details that need fixing with a full reread.

YOU'RE A WRITER: YOU GET TO MAKE UP WORDS

A reader of *The Frugal Editor* is likely to be someone who writes books or a freelancer who writes for periodicals who are sticklers for style choices, editing, and formatting. You might wear a different writing hat on different days. Regardless of what hat you're wearing, you need to know that the rules and guidelines for print and the Web are galaxies apart.

Think of them as different genres. The Web has adapted rules of its own that work very well on the screen but don't work so well on a printed page—or are just plain unacceptable to those in traditional publishing. The Web is *not* the place to find things to emulate—things like punctuation and style choices—if you are writing for literary journals or aiming for a professionally produced and edited book.

This is especially true for rules surrounding dashes, hyphens, em dashes, and en dashes. I had never heard of the last two before 1990. Until I started writing books and got into some formatting for my own books, I believed a dash is a dash is a dash, though I might not have written it in my head quite like that.

Because I am also a poet, I love fooling around with words. Sometimes I forego a hyphen and push words together to make one word or I attach them using a hyphen for a latch. Other times I make up entirely new ones like Lewis Carroll did when he wrote "Jabberwocky." As writers, we do not need to give up creative prerogatives, though we might be tempted because we see tons of rules for spelling, using dashes, and even how all these dashing little guys are formatted. What we read might be true, but each article tends to limit its advice to the way we use them in screen-only situations or in book- or print-only situations and it gets confusing. Thus, we might get bad advice for the project we are working on and not know it. Do we use spaces before and after em dashes or let them run right into the words or numbers on either side of them?

These choices were easy enough a few decades ago, but then came the Web and they started doing things with "dashes"—whatever they were using them for—to "help" us read more easily on a screen. Now it requires several paragraphs to explain how to format them for the different media and I do that at the end of this section.

Though new on-screen requirements compound a writer's problems, it was never easy. Someone made up the word *tick-tock* a long time ago. Is it one word or is it a hyphenated word? The answer in its most basic form: It is whatever the dictionary says it is unless you are trying to get a special meaning out of it. See the next sidebar to learn how to let Word's Spell Checker squiggles help you with the hyphen/two words dilemma.

In the poem on the next page, the word *good-bye* is an example of an intentionally hyphenated word that does not appear with a hyphen in any dictionary. It is from "Earliest Remembered Sound" in *Tracings* (bit.ly/CarolynsTracings), my award-winning chapbook of poetry published by Finishing Line Press and edited by Leah Maines.

> Father wears a military cap,
> grosgrain ribbons
> across his heart,
> smells of gabardine
> and good-byes.

I hyphenated *good-byes* because I wanted the careful reader (which readers of poetry tend to be) to see the poignant and positive quality in even a painful goodbye without explaining that in spite of the emotional upheaval surrounding the experience it was still a very *good* farewell. Poetry and writing teachers warn their students against being too expository. They advise us to trust our readers rather than preaching to them. To do that, we need access to all the tools of the trade rather than discarding some of the best because we want to be *right*.

Here is an example of putting two words together without a hyphen from "Everywhere My Dream," a poem in the same chapbook:

> I followed my childman
> beyond a young girl's borders
> calling nowhere home . . .

I felt using two words or hyphenating the word *childman* would not as powerfully illustrate the importance of the two entities—child and man—being of the same essence.

We have always formed new words by connecting two as if they were one (we kept that aspect of the German language even as English evolved away from its Germanic roots) or by attaching prefixes or suffixes to root words. As long as I can remember, prefixes have required us to make the one-word/hyphenated/two-word choices that drive us crazy. *Self-publishing* is one of those words that requires a hyphen, and it feels odd because, though *auto* means *self* in Latin, we do not use a hyphen when we precede a root word with *auto*. *Automobile* and *automatic* are examples. That's the beauty of dictionaries. Your dictionary should be a newer edition, because preferences seem to shapeshift.

If you have a good reason for putting two words together (like *shapeshift* in the paragraph above), have at it. You need a reason for your choice—a reason that can be articulated. Sometimes the reasons I hear from my students don't quite cut it. Reasons like "I just like it better that way," or worse, "I want to be different."

A caution in situations like this: You can drive yourself crazy checking several different dictionaries because you might get several answers. To help you with these conundrums, see the information box on the next page. Your computer's spell checker will help, but you'll probably get the most acceptable choice for your purpose if you use a reliable American dictionary (if you're in writing American English) or a reliable British dictionary like *Oxford* (if you're writing for the UK). At some point, you have to agree to disagree with someone. Our goal is to be our own best editor and to be equipped to reject another editor's take on our choice if she should try to undo our creativity. When that happens to me, though, it gives me pause. I consider that if she didn't quite get my brilliance, maybe others won't either. Rethinking choices is never a bad thing.

Here is how to force your spelling checker to give you better direction than it otherwise would: Push together two words you think might be one word or need a hyphen. Watch for that angry little red squiggle. *Oldfashioned* gets Word's red alert; *foolproof* doesn't. Yet both register as correct when left as two words.

Now try the same pair using a hyphen. Both *old-fashioned* and *fool-proof* come out with no squiggly notifier. The spelling checker helped in the first case but was wishy-washy in the second. Using *Merriam-Webster*, I'd choose *old-fashioned* and *foolproof*. You can see how Word hedges its bets before getting into the to-hyphenate-or-not-to-hyphenate fray.

Note: Words that seem like two but the dictionary lists as one can easily hide in your document. You don't notice them. Spell Checker doesn't either. Any pair of words that looks as if they might be remotely related should be shoved together as a test. You'll be asking Word to let you know what it thinks. Red squiggle? Let the words live separately. No red squiggle? Check in with Webster.

##

If you are not in your creative mode or in the mood to confound gremlins, see the next few information boxes that address the use of hyphens. When in doubt research like crazy, because stylebooks' guidelines are not always clear and hyphens are used (and not used) in so many ways. Be cautious when you approach gatekeepers, but beyond that, you need to be brave when you are in your poetic or literary mode.

MYRIAD USES FOR HYPHENS

Hyphens (-) can cause vitriolic arguments among otherwise tolerant people, and usually none of these combatants is 100% right because *choice* is part of the picture. Therefore, don't write to me to tell me I'm wrong. You are free to disagree. My only firm rule is to research the subject and the individual occurrence before using a hyphen and to be open to a different opinion (but not submissive to that opinion). On some things—even when we are trying to impress gatekeepers—there is no such thing as a zero-tolerance rule in spite of what strict grammarian Lynne Truss would have us believe in her *Eats, Shoots & Leaves* (bit.ly/ShootsLeaves) grammar book. There is, however, a best-choice rule to get you through the gatekeepers' iron gates.

Because the rules of hyphenating are so intricate and because even the experts disagree, the hyphen gremlin (one of the most spiteful of his species) knows that he can have a field day with them. Use your computer's find tool to pick up all the words with hyphens as a check, but do not rely on it. This is where you must do the hard work in manual mode. The next sidebar is a rundown of uses for hyphens; you know most of them, but give them a read anyway, won't you? Just to keep the gatekeepers on your side.

These are the more flexible rules for hyphens:

- You may occasionally ignore hyphens to make completely new words for clarity or creativity. We talked about how to do that in this chapter.
- Use hyphens to separate syllables in long words so the lines in your copy are of a more even length. We don't usually do this ourselves anymore because Word and other programs wrap lines for us. If you have a publisher, their computer program does this kind of hyphenating automatically, so if you have added syllable breaks of your own, you will only confuse it. The only time I break words myself is when I want to avoid what I call *gaposis* in fully justified copy for my Web site, for fliers, or occasionally when I format my self-published books.
- Use hyphens to separate some prefixes from root words. Your most trusted dictionary is the best go-to guy to learn when to use one, when to leave the prefix as a separate word, and when to let the prefix and root word cozy up to one another.
- Many grammarians say that when a *common* prefix is attached to a word there is no need for a hyphen. That includes prefixes like *co* or

Cont'd

post, regardless of how often you've seen *coauthor* with a hyphen. The *preferred* spelling is without one.

- Because there are so few *firm* rules governing prefixes, go for the choice that feels right or makes the meaning of the word you *invented* clearer.
- Most authorities agree: When you attach a prefix to a word like *antidefamation* that is *not* listed in the dictionary with that prefix, there is *no* need to use a hyphen. Beware! Word's spell checker often does not agree with the experts.
- Do not use hyphens to separate suffixes from root words. Just to make the subject more confusing, there might be a time when using a hyphen with suffixes will clarify your meaning. *Business-ese* is an example. I chose to use the hyphen in this word for this book. I adapted (made up?) the word anyway and it seemed better with the hyphen than without, perhaps because of the closely related *z* and *s* sounds. I chose to go with my own assessment for clarity over the rulebook. An editor might indeed be watching but I already had a publisher for the first edition of this book so worrying about gatekeepers was not an issue and the second edition is self-published. Obviously there *are* some advantages to independent publishing, especially for those of us with . . . mmmm . . . strong opinions.

Cont'd

SIDEBAR
Cont'd: Peek-a-Boo with Hyphens

- Don't use hyphens with double adjectives when one of them is a comparative like *well* or a superlative like *most*. I used *most trusted dictionary* earlier in this sidebar. You didn't miss the hyphen in *most trusted* because those words didn't need one. Another example: She is a *well known* author. Word gives you a blue squiggle alert because it doesn't want to take a stand. I will. Most trusted stylebooks tell us *not* to use the hyphen.

Some less flexible rules:
- Use a hyphen when attaching a prefix to a number or capitalized word. Examples: *Pre-1920s. Pre-Thanksgiving.*
- A typesetter makes a big deal of using a longer hyphen when adding a prefix to multiword compounds. You don't need to do that. A hyphen will do. Post World War II would become Post-World War II. These shorter dashes are also used for designating periods of years: *1980-1990.* They are also used to indicate opposition. An example: *urban-agrarian.*
- Use a hyphen when attaching a prefix to a word that is already hyphenated. My favorite grammar expert June Casagrande gives the example *non-self-serving.*

Cont'd

- When your hyphenated word shoves two vowels together, separate them with a hyphen (-).

  Example: *co-action*.

  Exceptions: Commonly used words like *cooperate* and *coauthor* mentioned above.

- Attach the prefix *non* to nouns. It is *nonsensical* and *nonsmoker*. This rule is easy to remember because we writers often use the word *nonfiction*. You do spell it that way, don't you? Unfortunately, there are always a few exceptions. *Non sequitur* is one of them. Even Word's Spell Checker knows that!

- Proper nouns *do* take a hyphen. It is *non-Mormon* and *non-Catholic*. Or you can say something like ". . . those who aren't Catholic."

- Avoid the hyphen when you want to connect a *ly* adverb to another word like "firmly tied knot."

  If you don't recall how to let your computer's spell checker help you determine whether a hyphen between words is preferred, go back to the sidebar on page 168 for tips. But remember those tips only help. Stylebooks and dictionaries should have the last word. When they disagree, you have the last word based on what you know about the genre you are writing in or the medium you are writing for.

##

As long as we are on the subject of dashes and hyphens, here are some general guidelines for formatting them both for print and the Net. To make it easy, let's pretend like the Web and books are fussy people who like different things.

Books are traditional folks. They like their hyphens (-) and em dashes (—) to fit comfortably between the letters right next to them—snuggle right up to them, as you see in this book.

The Web lives in a glaring environment and it wants you to keep your eyes on the screen as long as possible. It is a visual sort of guy. It likes lots of open space in its design *and* in its copy. It asks you to stick spaces—little visual cushions—on either side of dashes and related punctuations. Think (space)emdash(space) or (space)hyphen(space). Skip the spaces when you use a dash between numbers to indicate a timespan or series of pages. It is *1912-1914* or pages *3-30*—even on the Web.

WHAT ABOUT THOSE DOUBLE ADJECTIVES?

Double adjectives are not as tricky as they first seem. Some of us use them frequently when we write the words *self-published* book. *Self* modifies the word published, not the word *book*. Thus, we use a hyphen between the words. *Soft white clouds* might be interpreted two ways. *Soft* might modify clouds but it might also modify *white*. What is your meaning? We generally make up our minds about double adjectives based on reason. Here is an example of how to analyze your hyphen dilemma:

- If you are a poet and you want the reader to think about the softness of the color *white*—not how the *clouds* would feel if you reached out to touch them—use the hyphen. "The children lay on their backs observing the soft-white clouds."

- If you are describing the puffy quality of clouds *and* their whiteness, forget the hyphen. In this case, you would use a comma instead: "The children lay on their backs observing the soft, white clouds."
- A poet might take poetic license and make it softwhite clouds.

SIDEBAR
Quick Test for Hyphenating Adjectives

Here's a test for hyphenating multiple adjectives. Mentally place an *and* between the two adjectives you are considering. If it feels right, both adjectives modify the noun and no hyphen is needed.

Example: If you can say, "He is an exacting *and* proud editor," forget the hyphen. The editor is both *exacting* and *proud*. It becomes, "He is an exacting, proud editor." You could consider keeping the *and* instead. There is a difference—subtle, but different.

Example: When you can say, "He is a detail and oriented editor," you feel in your bones that *detail* describes *oriented.* It becomes "He is a detail-oriented editor."

Avoid using a hyphen when you feel inclined to connect an adverb that ends in *ly* to another word. June Casagrande, author of *The best punctuation book. Period* (http://bit.ly/PunctuationBook). and the syndicated newspaper column *A Word Please*, uses *happily married couple* as an example. The idea is that *ly* lets you know *happily* is already married (as it were) to the word *married*. You need add nothing more to make it so.

> **Note**: For a more rigid take on hyphens or if you are writing for UK readership, read Lynne Truss's *Eats, Shoots & Leaves, The Zero Tolerance Approach to Punctuation* (bit.ly/ShootsLeaves). She is a Brit and the British publishers follow different grammar, spelling, and style rules from those in the US. The publishers of the Harry Potter books even set up their own American editions so they wouldn't confuse young American readers.

BLAMING THE NET, THE MEDIA, AND EVEN LINGUISTICS

Sometimes I think the world is against us writers. Certainly the Net brought us new language, new formatting, new design—and not all the newbies are bad. Languages have always been influenced from the street up. By movies. Later by TV. They often contribute to a more colorful language. Sometimes to a more flexible language. They're a little like marriages; their influence can be for better or for worse.

Languages have always been fluid, only one of the reasons writers have to be on guard against anything and anyone who might be cousins to the gremlins. We need to watch for whatever dilutes and weakens. We need to stand against anything that obfuscates. Wordiness. Grammatical degenerations. Clichés that begin to get on our nerves. What is candy to texters and surfers can be subtle career killers for the rest of us.

Writers are the guardians of our language—or should be. We have a stake in protecting it. We are hired to do jobs that people with very good command of the English language cannot do because they don't know as much about it as we do. Have you ever wished that more companies would hire great tech writers to write or edit the instructions they put on the backs of their boxes or into the booklets for their electronic products? Some of us make our livings based on how well we foil gremlins.

I am on a vendetta against the misuse of the different forms of *to lie* and *to lay*—even among writers. Our culture considers it rude to correct others' English so we don't stand up in the middle of a yoga class and scream how nice it would be if our instructor could learn to tell us to *lie* down—a verb she must use every day. Therefore, I suffer silently when she tells us to *lay* down. Culturally, most English speakers are circumspect about correcting others' grammar. That's OK, but we don't have to exacerbate the problem with our writing.

Back to my lie/lay harangue. We all know *to lie* and *to lay* are different verbs. I could write an entire booklet on this subject alone. Let's hope this simplification helps:

The verb *to lie* does not take a direct object.
The verb *to lay* does.

Therefore, if there is a direct object, use *lay/laid/laid*. Problems arise because the past tense of *to lie* is the same as the present tense of *to lay* and because almost everyone uses the verb *to lie* incorrectly in casual conversation (yes, even TV anchors and yoga teachers). If the direct object rule doesn't help, maybe this will:

- You *lie* out in the sun to get a tan (no direct object). If the action is in the past, you say, "Yesterday I *lay* out in the sun." With a helping verb it is "I *have lain* out in the sun every day since the first of May."

- You tell your dog, "*Lie* down, Fido."

- Using the verb *to lie* correctly feels comfortable enough eventually, but most feel self-conscious saying *have, has,* or *had lain.* So work around those tenses that require helping verbs. It's easy. Use another verb like *have relaxed* or rearrange the time requirements of the paragraph you are writing.

Note: *To rise* and *to raise* are similar to *to lie* and *to lay. To raise* requires a direct object. *To rise* doesn't. We *raise* the blind in the morning. The sun *rises* in the morning.

Just to be clear, fiction writers or those who write anecdotes can use *lie* and *lay* incorrectly in dialogue and in internal thought. They might even use it in narrative that comes from a specific point of view—the point of view of a person who wouldn't know the difference. Maybe you can use one of the tricks Wally Lamb uses in his *We Are Water* published by HarperCollins (bit.ly/WeAreWater) to make it feel OK.

He lets the character herself doubt her own grammatical expertise. Or another character notices her . . . uh . . . poor grammar skills. Sometimes Lamb juxtaposes the improper usage against the verbiage of a character who knows how to say it right.

Here is a short list of some words that can be a danger to your reputation. They are the ones I see most often in the editing I do. We often use them in our creative work and in the marketing of our books.

Bad, **Badly**. Many try so hard to get this right that they get it wrong. When you feel bad, *bad* is not an adverb. In the sentence, "I feel bad," *bad* modifies *I* and is an adjective. It is known as a predicate adjective because it comes after the verb, but it is still an adjective. Unless your sense of touch has been damaged (almost never!), you *feel* bad. It's too bad English teachers don't teach diagramming these days, for a good diagram makes this quirk of the English language very clear. You can *do* something (like play ball) badly, but it's a rare thing indeed to need to say that your sense of touch (I feel badly) is out of whack.

All right, never **alright**. This is a true rule in the United States, and shunning *alright* may help avoid the ire of gatekeepers everywhere. What if your teenybopper character spouts the word and runs the two together? You might choose the latter but is the risk of raising the dander of an editor worth it when they sound the same regardless of how they are spelled?

Quote, **Quotation**. When you are discussing endorsements and blurbs with agents, you might be required to use the words *quote* and *quotation*. That makes it especially important that you know how to use them. I borrowed this directly from one of the tips in my *SharingwithWriters* newsletter:

> "**Grammar Tip**. Many writers use the words *quotation* and *quote* interchangeably. They are not interchangeable. Quote is a verb that means to repeat the words of a writer or speaker. Think of it as *to quote. Quotation* is a noun. It means that which is quoted (the words)."

ISBN stands for International Standard Book Number. To add the word *number* or the number symbol (#) is redundant. Ditto for ASIN and other initialisms used to identify books by the publishing industry.

Awhile, A while. People often confuse the adverb *awhile* with the noun phrase *a while*, especially when *a while* comes after a preposition. Prepositions need objects, so because *a while* has a noun in it, you write *after a while, for a while, in a little while*.

Only. There are only three golden rules for *only*! 1. Be sure this word is needed. 2. Be sure it is placed in the sentence so it modifies the word or idea you want it to. 3. Don't overuse it.

Regardless, never **irregardless**, unless you are writing dialogue for a character who tries to sound smarter by throwing extra syllables into words. Here are a couple of others that the snobbery gremlin works hard at insinuating into our language:

- *Cohabitate* when *cohabit* will work, ahem . . . better.

- *Orientate*d for *oriented.*
- *Preventative* for *preventive. Preventative* is a second choice in most dictionaries, not listed in others.
- My personal least favorite is *signage.* Some dictionaries don't agree with me because it is now so commonly used. *Signage* is unnecessary and sounds as if the word has a stuffy nose. Plain old *signs* functioned well for centuries before somebody tried to sound official.

Already, **All ready**. *Already* is an adverb that means previously—it has to do with time. *All ready* is an adjective phrase that means prepared or in a state of readiness.

> **Note**: There is one *l* in already. "I have already completed the first draft." (However, as your editor, I would probably suggest you consider cutting both the *already* and the *have* from your copy).

Spitting image. This phrase is a bastardization of *spit and image.* Most readers will not catch your point if you choose to use it in dialogue to characterize a person who isn't in the know, so why run the risk of using it?

People, **Persons**. *People* is the plural of *person* and is preferred. Writers seem to get self-conscious when they write cover letters, query letters, and media releases; their discomfort shows when they use *persons.* In *Webster's Tenth New Collegiate Dictionary*, *persons* isn't given its own entry.

Enormity, **Enormous**. Enormity means bad, not big, at least among the literate. So sayeth the *Chicago Manual of Style* (bit.ly/ChiStBk) and most other arbiters of language. If you want *big*, use *big*, *large*, or *enormous*. *Humongous* is slang but *enormity* is just plain wrong.

Titled, **Entitled**. Here is a word choice you will almost certainly need to make, especially when you are talking about your book in media releases, query letters, book proposals, your Web site, your media kit. Yikes! *Entitled* is not the same as *titled*. Yep, we can use *entitle* to mean give a title to something but it does not refer to the title itself. In your query letters, please say something like, "My memoir is *titled* [your title here]." It is incorrect to say, "I am submitting the first three chapters of my new novel *entitled* [your title here]." Not only that, but it sounds overly formal, labored, and downright annoying.

Effete means worn out, not snobbish. When Spiro Agnew was Vice President of the United States, he famously used the word but he probably did not expect readers to interpret it to mean snobbish. He was doing whatever he could to insult those "nabobs of negativity," for no one wants to be *tired* and he had already used other deprecatory adjectives that indicated they might be snobs.

Myriad. You do not need the *a* and the *of* when you use the term as an adjective. It is unlikely that you will be called on it, but plain old *myriad* will do. "Editing presents myriad challenges" is correct.

Since, **Because**. Maybe someone saw *since* used interchangeably with *because* and liked the look or sound of it. Maybe he thought it added variety to our speech where it wasn't needed. Since then, writers have been using it when *because* would be more accurate. Use *since* when referring to a period of time. Use *because* when giving a reason for something.

Literally, Figuratively. People often slur the word literally and make it "litally" or "literrrrly." You might wonder what this has to do with writing. Many writers are speakers, too, and this is a word that comes up among authors a lot. A publisher once mentioned that *literally* is often used in book proposals when the writer means *figuratively*. June Casagrande, grammar guru, used this as an example for how *not* to do it: "They were literally glued to their seats." June, with her ever-present humor, notes that someone would have applied glue to either the chair or their posterior if that situation were, indeed, *literal*.

Guess what. *Guess what* is not a question. It's a command. A period after the phrase will do just fine.

Between and other prepositions. Most of us use pronouns after a preposition correctly. *To him, over her, on me*. It seems that otherwise perfectly literate authors (like all of us) get self-conscious when writing to gatekeepers who hold our fates in their hands, but this is no time to get high falutin'. *Between* is a preposition. We say "Between you and *me*," not "Between you and *I*," even if the latter sounds more . . . well, literate. Use caution in selecting your pronoun wherever you have a compound pronoun but especially after that troublesome preposition *between*.

Try and, Try to. To keep your copy criticism-free, use *try to*. *Try and* is not wrong, only casual, but if a gatekeeper notices, she won't give you a chance to make your point.

Snuck. Yes, there is such a word. A very ugly one, don't you think? Dictionary.com says, "Many writers and editors have a lingering unease about the form, particularly if they recall its nonstandard origins." Sixty-seven percent disapproved of *snuck* in surveys, but this is not the time to flex your tolerance for the colloquial. Let's be cautious here—for the preservation of our reputations and to assure the success of our submissions. Avoid *snuck* unless you are writing dialogue for teens in detention at Central High. I mean, even the Simpsons prefer the more standard *sneaked*.

Serial Commas. Many disagree about whether or not to put a comma after the item that comes just before the *and* (or other conjunctions) in a series. Serial commas are *de rigueur* for traditionally published books. Academics usually use them in dissertations and other formal writing. Journalists and publishers of nonfiction often choose *not* to use them. I rarely abide by the Associated Press's (AP) preference for skipping serial commas because occasionally they can make the difference between clarity and confusion. Besides, one more comma can't use up that much more ink.

Numbers, Numerals. The difference between these is only important for academics or those who write books. Did you know that the style rules for using numerals (or, conversely, writing out numbers) in books differ from those in other print media? No, I'm not jerking you around here. Use the *Chicago Manual of Style* (bit.ly/ChiStBk) to learn different rules for your novel from rules you use for your chatty blog. Rules for novels are simpler and stricter: Write out numbers that start a sentence and all the others from one to one hundred—anywhere they are needed. For nonfiction, write out numbers above ten and make a style choice for numbers over ten. For those who want to be exact:

- *23* is a numeral.
- *Twenty-three* is a number.
- You can have a *number* of friends or *23* friends or twenty-three friends, but you can't have a *numeral* of friends.

Find more wordtrippers—a whole booklet more—in my *Great Little Last-Minute Editing Tips for Writers* (bit.ly/Last-MinuteEditing). It is an addendum to this section of *The Frugal Editor*. It is meant as a quick brushup and I hope to write another as I find more trippers to help you avoid the ire of gatekeepers.

WORDINESS, CLICHÉS, AND A FEW POLITICALLY CORRECT GUIDELINES

It is impossible to cover wordiness, clichés, and politically correct use in anything other than a complete reference book on these subjects. I hope the few in this section encourage you to keep thinking about wordiness and about what is politically correct (and whether or not you want to *be* politically correct). We become so accustomed to some phrases and constructions that we don't realize that they are unnecessary, that they contribute to more wordiness and more convoluted sentence structures, and that they might give our readers a wrong impression.

Tuning into wordiness

Perfectly good phrases seem to creep into our lives, take hold, and become clichés of the most annoying kind. Here are a few examples that might help you spot emerging wordiness and lower your tolerance level for them.

At the end of the day. We hear this phrase on any news segment on any given day over and over again—even on highly respected (and scripted!) news programs like CBS's *60 Minutes*. Of course, this phrase has its place, but when it is repeated *ad infinitum,* it becomes annoying. *End of the day* does nothing that a future tense will not do except add pomposity to the occasion—and a few extra words. It is more noxious when we use *end of the day* metaphorically so it has nothing to do with being specific about time.

Moving forward. This is a first cousin to *at the end of the day*. There is generally no need for it when tense already points to the future. Its use has begun to feel as if correspondents and anchors like to hear themselves talk and it usually detracts from otherwise professional presentations.

Boots on the ground is overused, too. Don't even get me started on that one. Those poor soldiers with no discernible bodies wearing those boots.

The reason for. Phrases like this are often clutter and they sound as if you don't have confidence in your own convictions. There are times when you want to sound that way, but don't use them if you want to instill confidence in your expertise. You can usually just eliminate the phrase or supplant it with *because*.

In order to. In order to cut the crap, cut the words *in order* and maybe the *to* as well. Here are examples:
- "Study grammar in order to foil the gremlins" may be edited to read, "Study grammar to foil the gremlins."
- You may also invert the clauses: "To foil gremlins, study grammar."

The fact that. This wordy construction can be trimmed in a similar way to editing *in order to*.

Due to, Because of. We often see *due to* when *because* would be more accurate. *Because of* and *due to* both encourage passive, awkward construction. Here is an example and its cure. Notice the edit requires a bit of rearranging.

Example: "The author's loss of a contract was *due* *to* her poor grammar." **Edit**: "Poor grammar cost the author her contract." This edit gets rid of *due to* and does it without substituting *because of*. The trick? Simply using a stronger verb than *was*. Yay!

Reach out. Instead of saying, "We reached out," just say, "We asked . . . ." It avoids a phrase that has become a bit of a cliché and it is more direct. R*each out* has a touchy-feely connotation we may not need . . . or want. When we avoid getting into a wordy mode, gremlins have a tougher time getting hold of our brains and hanging on.

I run a series of wordy phrases, overused phrases, and just plain annoying constructions in my *Frugal, Smart, and Tuned-In Editor* blog

(TheFrugalEditor.blogspot.com). I also post essays on politically correct terms that become cumbersome or defy reason (keep reading for a little more on that subject). Please subscribe *and* submit guest posts for consideration. I include credits complete with your books' titles and links to your books' buy pages when you contribute.

Dangerous political curves ahead

The most glaring politically incorrect *faux pas* occur in discussions about race and ethnicity. Let's use the term *African American* as a benchmark for other situations. Different stylebooks offer different guidelines but all their suggestions can inform the choices we make for our own writing. Most suggest:

- The word *black* be used as an adjective and that *a black* be replaced by *a black person*.
- You should hyphenate *African-American* when it is used as a modifier. An *African-American diplomat*. *African American* (without a hyphen) should be reserved for use as a noun.
- It is safe to use these guidelines in similar situations including *German American*, *Asian American*, etc.

The *LA Times'* stylebook suggests we adjust terminology if a person we're writing about has a preference. That seems only considerate.

Many like Paula Deen got themselves into touchy situations because they were insensitive to what is politically correct, ignorant of how to avoid politically incorrect language, or their language actually reflects their personal bigotry. A litany of other topics demands scrutiny before clicking a send button. Among them are mental capability, handicaps of all kinds (often called *challenges*), religion, and gender. Even *Happy Holidays* and *Merry Christmas* can stir up controversy.

Sometimes we *must* use terms that were once widespread but are unacceptable today. As an example, the film *Twelve Years a Slave* requires the use of the n-word to achieve authenticity. We must carefully research sensitive issues and examine our own intent, goals, and the artistic needs of our work. What we needn't do is fall into politically correct (PC) traps where some try to coopt certain terms for their own agenda or disparage them without giving full consideration to why a writer might have used them.

THE DREADED CLAUSE INTRODUCERS

So what exactly are *clause introducers*? In my effort to avoid using grammar terms that turn innocent fourth graders into the kinds of people who shun diagramming (and editing), I made up the term. They are words like *that*, *which*, and *who*. They are like little hosts who introduce newcomer clauses to a party. Here is the short, easy lowdown.

- Accepted wisdom from *The American Heritage Book of English Usage* (bit.ly/AmerHeritage) says that *who* "is quintessential English usage, going back to the Old English period" and should be used exclusively when referring to human beings. The keyword here is *exclusively*. A few argue with such a respected tome, but I figure there is no reason to invite the wrath of even a few gatekeepers—primarily American ones—

who swear by the who rule. You have too much riding on it.

- Use *which* to introduce nondefining clauses, (clauses that give the reader *additional, nonessential* information). These are clauses you could pick up and throw in a trash heap without changing the main idea of the sentence and that nonessential quality is usually indicated by setting the clause apart with a comma.

- Use *that* to introduce clauses that identify whatever it refers to in the main part of the sentence. In this case, the clause it introduces gives *essential* meaning to the sentence.

Easy, huh? Nevertheless, we make it hard. Clause introducers usually don't give us much trouble except when we are deciding if we should use *that* or eliminate it. Many think the word *that* is a no-no, so they try to eliminate it unless it is necessary to understanding the sentence easily. Some are adamant about including *that* when the *subject* of the clause is different from the word or phrase the clause refers to.

Example: "Martin was reading the book *that* I was reading." *I* is the subject of the relative clause and *I* is nowhere to be found in the first part of the sentence. Instead, *that* refers to *book*, not to *Martin*, the subject of the independent clause.

Others like to take a red pen to *that*.

Example: "Martin was reading the book I was reading." This is a perfectly understandable sentence without *that*, but using *that* adds a little clarity, don't you think?

You get to choose, though journalists are more inclined to deep-six the *thats* than the editors of books.

Do know that even if you edit out *that* in an instance like this, it is still there. It is in hiding, something words do frequently in English. When they go undercover, they are understood by English speakers to be there—invisibly, but understood nonetheless.

Here are two examples that illustrate how clarity can be affected by hiding *that* or pretending it doesn't exist:

Examples:

With *that*: "The gremlins find *that* under these circumstances they can do their worst work."

Without *that*: "The gremlins find under these circumstances they can do their best work."

If you omit *that* as shown in the second example, the meaning is not clear. We might expect—for a moment at least—that the gremlins are going to find something unsavory hidden under those *circumstances* in the same way they might find a tooth under a pillow. It will take a minute for some readers to put themselves back on the rail of understanding. When we confuse readers—even for a second—we lose some of the momentum we are creating.

It seems fair to mention that we writers can find nourishing veggies in the new media *or* old. It's a good thing to separate the decay-producers (which shall go unmentioned) and the wholesome like *The New Yorker*, *The New York Times*, *The Smithsonian*, and literary and review journals like *Agni* and *The Missouri Review* where both broccoli and protein can be found. Whatever your preference—online or print—it might not hurt to make a point of reading more of the ones that do our writing bodies good. We might discover new writing techniques and examples of good grammar and structure that ingrain themselves into our subconscious. I *know* we will find inspiration.

Speaking of inspiration, I hope you are inspired to take from this book what you have learned (or been reminded of) about editing to whatever task you're working on in this moment.

If you are ready for the final housekeeping phase of your manuscript edit (that is coming up next!), I know new techniques and refreshed skills will come in handy.

SECTION SIX

FINAL HOUSECLEANING

CHAPTER FIFTEEN
YOU'RE B-A-A-A-CK FOR YOUR
TWO FINAL, MANUAL EDITS

I can't see you, but I know you are rolling your eyes or tapping your tired fingers. Manual edits and all those tricks with the computer aren't enough? You have two more edits to go before we talk about the professional way to submit your work to gatekeepers. When you finish that final housekeeping chore, you might not understand *why* what you have done is not sufficient, but you will know that it isn't.

Neither of these two final reads should be on your computer screen. Printing your manuscript on paper is not good for trees, so please use the backsides of recycled paper. Now the good news. You get to curl up and read your printout by a cozy fire or in a quiet corner of your favorite library.

NEXT-TO-LAST MANUAL EDIT FOR PROFESSIONAL CONSUMPTION

For this edit, you want a different perspective of your manuscript so you can see it anew. Your first manual edits were on double-spaced manuscripts. Print out this one (the first of your final two) with single spaces because it will more closely resemble how it will look on a printed page that way. Here are the steps:

- Visually scan each page for odd spacing, paragraph indents, and anything else that offends your artistic sensibilities, and then read it once over in this format carefully. Use a colored pen for corrections. It will be easier on your tired eyes. I like using little precut Post-it notes, too. I guarantee that you will find errors during this read even after all the work you have done. When you are all through with this edit, make those corrections one at a time in your electronic copy. As you read, you will get a better feel for:
    - Transitions, character, time, location and setting.
    - Flow.
    - Dialogue patterns.
    - Typos.
    - Misuse of synonyms, homonyms, and other closely aligned words. I read a friend's book that had been in release for over a year and the copy confused the words *metal* and *medal* throughout the book. Not one editor, reviewer, agent, or reader had mentioned it to him. He hopes no one noticed.
    - Unnecessary repetition. Yes, even after the electronic search! Some repetition may be necessary, especially if your reader is likely to reread some segments later, but axe the rest.
    - How your chapter titles, chapter divisions, subtitles, and the other two-by-fours that frame your book are working. The formatting of these dividers must be

consistent throughout your book, including spacing between lines, between letters, and between words.

- You'll be responsible for an index if you're self-publishing nonfiction, but your editor may ask you to provide one if you are publishing traditionally, too. Either way, you'll have to hire it done or take on the project yourself. Now is the time to jump on it and highlight keywords important to your overall vision. Even a professional editor will appreciate that input.
- When you are done with this edit, make corrections one at a time in your electronic copy.

Now your manuscript is presentable, it is ready to be read by a few people who are willing to give you feedback, people who will help you polish it. For your protection, mark copies you give to others "Advance Reader's Copy" and include a disclaimer that the manuscript is not fully edited in case it should appear in public sometime in the future. Here are ideas for people who can help with this effort. Ask them to go over your manuscript for you.

- Enlist fellow critique group members or have a writing friend help.
- Get help from coworkers who are experts in the subject you are writing about. They are not really reviewing your book in the traditional bookish sense; these are critiques from colleagues who can spot errors where you left out essential information or where information is inaccurate. This process, called a peer review, is often used in academia to assure accuracy. If peers find

anything major, you might need another revision and edit.

> **Note**: Peer reviews are usually used for nonfiction or academic work, but if I were writing a crime novel, I would ask a mystery writer like Linda Morelli to help me with her extensive knowledge of forensics. Or a detective. Or a doctor. Whatever the book seems to require. This kind of feedback can be helpful if you are writing in a new genre, too.

- Ask a few friends who read widely in whatever genre you write in for their input. Let them watch for typos, but encourage them to comment on anything that might occur to them. However, remember they are readers, not experts. Weigh their ideas accordingly. If using amateur editors is new to you, be wary of those who overreach to the point of wanting to restyle or even rewrite your book. Give each of your helpmates some guidelines (see below), but if they overstep, don't take offense. This is your creation. Accept what you can use and discard the rest. Be equally wary of being so set in your ways that you don't listen. Give each reader a list of things to watch for. Questions you might ask include:
  - Is there anything in the book they don't understand?
  - Did they stop reading (or want to stop) at a given place?

- Is there information they would like to know that didn't turn up—at least by the end of the book?
- Questions can be general or specific—something like, "What would you say the '59 Ford in this novel is a metaphor for." If no one gets it, consider why not, but before you make changes ask your fellow writers the same questions. The concepts of *metaphor* or *symbol* might not be something your general readers consider when they read.

When you get your readers' comments back, you will have input from fresh new eyes and new viewpoints to consider. You will have at least one reader's input, an expert's input, and at least one professional writer's suggestions.

Having these edits done simultaneously saves time, though you might find that linear input gives better results because edits layered on top of edits you have made might be more finely tuned.

If your reader is comfortable with computers, let him or her edit using the Tracker in your word processing program (See instructions on how to use TRK in Chapter Nine, "Use Word's Tools, Don't Trust Them"). Use Track's color-coding feature explained there so you know who made specific suggestions.

Note: Don't forget to add these helpers' names to your acknowledgments. Each will appreciate a signed complimentary copy upon the book's release. It is the least you can do. If you feel confident that they like your book, you can also ask them to mention the book or their reading experience on Facebook and Twitter as part of your prepublishing marketing effort.

YOUR FINAL, FINAL EDIT

By now, you probably realize there is no such thing as a final, final edit. You will keep finding things to change as long as you continue to reread your manuscript—or most any other document for that matter. You will keep finding things to improve as long as you keep learning. We sometimes need someone else to tell us when to quit. That is usually once our book is in print, but because e-books are so easy to update, that is changing. Regardless, you owe your book one more go-through before it goes out for general readership.

Do not look at your book during this time you are getting input from fellow writers, general readers, and colleagues as part of your last edit. You will be so antsy you won't want to wait. Still, you will be glad you slowed the process at this stage. Doing another read-through before your brain has had time to relax is a big mistake. You want to be truly ready for the final, final edit. When you are, you'll love finding hardly a single thing that needs to be taken care of.

Print your manuscript using double spaces between the lines this time. Double-spaced manuscripts are easier to read and that is the format you use when you submit to traditional publishers and agents. The exceptions may be nonfiction with lots of images; in that case, save to a .pdf file instead. Your query or cover letter and other marketing/selling tools will be sent to agents, editors, and others single spaced, so editing these once with plenty of space between lines will work to your advantage. It is also a good idea to read aloud this time.

Apply this process to anything you send out into the light of the world. That includes your manuscript, query or cover letters, media kit, media releases, and book proposals. Even Web site copy. The list is endless. For more information on getting promotional material right, see my *The Frugal Book Promoter* (bit.ly/FrugalBookPromo).

These final read-throughs are needed for a couple of reasons. Gremlins were working on your manuscript as you were editing (they never sleep) and the cleaner the copy, the more likely you are to see the abstruse and ordinary errors that were hidden before.

ARE YOU CONVINCED THAT YOU STILL DON'T NEED AN EDITOR?

If after all this hard work you think your editing is done and you don't need to partner with an editor, I understand. You may rationalize that you will hand your manuscript over to a publisher who will assign one of theirs to you.

On the other hand, all this work might convince you that you *do* need an editor. You might realize that you have only scratched the surface. Certainly you will see that an extra pair of eyes (sharp eyes) and an extra set of professional skills (skills rooted in lots of experience) can make a difference for your book.

Perhaps you decide to small-press-, or subsidy-publish (where you pay someone to do the publishing for you). In those situations, the likelihood of having an accomplished editor assigned to you is not very high. I know many authors published by *big* presses who were not impressed with the expertise of their editors. If that turns out to be the case, this section will help you find a good editor and the rest of this book will make a better writer of you and help you partner with your editor, no matter how you acquired him or her.

Before you begin the hiring process, ask yourself if you will be open to suggestions. If not, then don't spend the money for a full edit. You might prefer to hire a proofreader. That should cost less.

You can sometimes tell what kind of an editor you are interviewing by how much he or she charges. If that is one dollar a page, expect that he or she might be getting started in the business or someone who checks only for elementary grammar and spelling errors and a few other tracks left by gremlins. If the fee is seven to ten dollars a page, you might get an edit but also explanations you can learn from.

The sad thing is that sometimes the fee is no indicator at all. That is why you should check the next information box on possible shams (or even outright scams) before you begin your search for an editor. Once you have narrowed your search to a handful, ask:

- Do they have experience editing works in the *same genre* as yours.
- If your book is nonfiction, will they check its organization or give you suggestions for content?
- If your book is fiction, will they give you suggestions regarding motivation, character development, and other aspects of craft like plot points, the big gloom, and denouement. This kind of input can make a difference for your book's success.

- Do they supply references? (See more on how to make references work for you in the sidebar below.)
- Do they charge by the hour, the page, the job?
- Ask each to *estimate* the cost of editing your book. The editor might request a copy of your manuscript to give you a meaningful estimate and you should ask for a cap on additional fees.
- Will these editors supply you with lists of their edited books and other credentials? Are they associated with a writers' department at a university?
- During this interview process, try to determine if your personalities mesh well.
- Can they edit synopses? Book proposals? Having knowledge of book marketing is helpful but not essential.

SIDEBAR
How to Avoid Internet Shams and Scams

- Ask instructors/professors who teach in the writing department at your local university for their recommendations. Not the English department but the writing department or program. Ask what published books they edited.
- Ask the directors of the best writing conferences (again, preferably those associated with universities or colleges) for their suggestions. Then ask if they have seen any of the editor's work.

Cont'd

- Beware the Web—at least, beware of using only a search engine to find an editor. Many of the editors recommended by professionals will have their own Web sites, of course, but many self-styled "professionals" will, too.

  Note: Having written a book (self- or traditionally published) doth not magically make a writer into an editor. My beloved (and now deceased) editor had several decades of experience at several major university presses as well as scads of individual clients.

- Ask respected published authors, preferably those whose books you have read or those published by the most trusted of publishers, for their recommendations. Sometimes you can reach famous authors you don't know through the contact feature on their Web sites.
- Check the acknowledgment pages of books published by premier publishers. Many use stables of freelance editors and if an author has credited the editor, he or she might be open to editing your book.
- Do not select an editor based on the cheapest quote. You wouldn't do that if you were getting bids from a contractor to build a house for you, right?

Cont'd

- Do not hire an editor recommended by an agent who tells you they will only represent your book if you use (and pay for) their editor—or if you must pay the agent a fee for his editor's services.
- Sorry, but do not trust the editors at huge publish-on-demand presses, the ones that call you to enlist your business and charge you hefty fees. You might be assigned an editor who is adequate but your chances are not good.
- I said it before, but it bears repeating: *Even if someone you trust recommends an editor, ask for references from the editor.* And interview the recommended editor using the questions in this chapter as a guideline.

  Note: Getting references does you no good if you do not fact-check and research what you learn from this process.

  ##

When you ask professionals for referrals, ask pertinent questions, questions like:

- How does the professional *know* this editor? (The answer might be an indication they are cousins or best friends or in debt to one another.)
- Why does the professional recommend this editor over others? His preferences might be very

different from yours. Or you might learn about qualifications you never thought to ask about.

- What does the professional consider this editor's most important credential? You can tell a lot about the professional's standards by his answer to this question.

If your source is an author or publisher, be suspicious. Ask him or her these questions:

- Did the editor work on more than one of his or her books. If not, is that because the author found someone better, because the author wrote only one book, because the author changed genres, or because the editor was booked or had raised her rates?
- What kind of book or books did she edit for the author? (You are looking for an editor with experience in your genre.)
- Did the editor get defensive if the author chose not to follow a suggestion?
- Did the editor explain her suggestions to the author?
- Did the editor listen to this person's questions and concerns?

If you want to hire an editor but are worried about the cost, factor in the value of what private or university classes that cover structure and technique would cost you. That is what you will be getting with an editor who explains their edits, including the differences between style choices and grammar rules, help with writing technique and structure, and one who goes a step beyond what they promised.

Example: A ten-week class at UCLA can run about $600 plus parking and gasoline or a total of about $800 each. You teacher's attention will be divided and you will probably need more than one class. Universities have a whole catalog to choose from! Or you'll need a master class that can be even more expensive. If you subtract that amount from what a top-tier, educate-as-you-go, first-choice, editor would charge you—say, $12 for each page of twelve point, double-spaced copy—you may decide the cost of a full-service editor and hand-holder is more targeted to your needs, takes less time, and costs less than several classes.

These guidelines may not seem easy, but trust me, following them can save you more time and headaches in the long run than it takes to read and follow them. Do know that they are similar to the ones huge corporations use to save themselves from making costly errors. Once you have chosen your editor, given them time to do a great job, and accepted or rejected her suggestions, you are on the way. Your proof copy or galley edit is up next. Be prepared for some big surprises. At least they won't be shockers because you have this book in your hands.

CHAPTER SIXTEEN
THE GALLEY EDIT—WHERE YOU COME TO BELIEVE IN GREMLINS

You wrote and edited your manuscript and submitted it. You wrote and edited your query letter and sent it out. An agent or publisher loved your book. Yay! You worked (maybe haggled) with your editor. Perhaps you decided to self- or subsidy-publish. Now your galleys or proofs are at your door. This is your last chance to edit and, believe me, the gremlins will have done their silent work because the manuscript has been in the hands of someone else—maybe even another computer program. So don't get lax now.

Diane Newton, editor of *Secrets II*, an anthology of stories about the "human condition dark secrets kept or revealed," says somehow the galleys for that book didn't have "a single word in italics after page sixty-three, and . . . there are fifty places that need italics in the last three stories and just about as many in the backmatter, including authors' bios." She says she had never before needed more than eight galley changes.

We hope there will be few if any galley changes because changes beget more errors and because anything missed in this final state will almost certainly slip into print. No wonder Diane was upset. One hundred or more corrections is a chore. Even when you are oh so thorough, the gremlins can getcha. It is worse, though, if you must blame yourself instead of our tricky nemeses with purple warts.

TRICKS TO FOIL THE GALLEY GREMLINS

This is your last stand against the gremlins. You can win. Use all the skills you have learned.

When your galley or proof book arrives, edit it and don't turn the corrections in. Let them sit around until just before your deadline. During this down time, don't look at the book or the correction sheet or whatever method your publisher asks you to use.

In the meantime, let another pair of eyes—preferably a fresh pair—do a galley check, too.

Just before you e-mail or ship your galleys back for the last (gasp!) time, read the galley once again. This time out loud. Poets might read lines from the bottom of each stanza to the top and other writers can adapt this method to their genre. Reading backwards slows you down. Bet you find at least one more track left by a gremlin.

Most publishers and editors use programs like Word's Tracker for editing. You'll find more information on this tool in this book. Check the Index and read all the entries for *tracker* listed there.

Still, some still prefer to edit by hand. If you receive a physical galley marked up with symbols you don't understand (usually in red pencil), learn more about proofreading marks at this site: merriam-webster.com/mw/table/proofrea.htm. Journalists know these symbols. Teachers often use them. Writers of all kinds find them handy to know.

Check up on your formatter

I know I cautioned you about never trusting your computer. Or your publisher. Or the best, smartest, most detail-oriented editor around. Ditto for formatters who do the nitty-gritty like pagination.

The best formatters appreciate working with an author who has some knowledge of the formatting process so they won't mind questions or input. It makes their job easier and saves them time.

Remember my friend Kathe Gogolewski? She found that an arcane formatting rule lost some points for her story when she entered it in a contest. Here are some other formatting essentials you need to know more about when submitting a manuscript:

- You might need to suggest to your publisher or formatter that each chapter should start about one-third of the way down the page—specifically the page on the right (or the odd-numbered page). This space is called sinkage and it was once part of the job of a publisher's book designer. Many small publishers do not *have* book designers these days. Thus, your publisher or designer or formatter might not remember or know this is something readers have come to expect. Or they want to save space, paper, or money (long books tend to cost more to produce). When you enter your book in a contest (something strongly suggested by many book marketers like me), a departure like this will be noticed. Can you imagine missing the Pulitzer by two points? Further, your readers will subconsciously be aware of cramped pages. My cover designer, Chaz DeSimone (desimonedesign.com/) says, "White space at the beginning of each chapter gives readers a breather, a sort of intermission."

- Each chapter should begin on an odd-numbered page unless your text is particularly long. One of the few universal publishing rules is that odd numbers are right-hand pages. That might mean that a blank or nearly blank page appears in your galley. It will most often be the page opposite (on the left) from the beginning of each chapter, but blanks can legitimately occur in front and backmatter, too. If a blank page—which should not be given a page number even though it is counted in your book's final page count—doesn't fit one these descriptions, bring it to the attention of your formatter or publisher and check to see how it looks when you receive your proof copy.

- E-book font shouldn't be smaller than ten point. (See this book's Appendix Six for instructions on e-book formatting.) Twelve-point Times New Roman is a safe choice for print.

- Watch for widows. A widow is a single line— often the last line of a paragraph—that is separated from its related text and appears by itself at the top of the next printed page or column.

- Watch for orphans. An orphan is a heading, subheading, or a single line of a paragraph separated from its related text that appears at the bottom of a printed page or column. Use a page break to force Word to put it at the top of the next page with its related text. You will eventually notice both orphans and widows easily if you train yourself to watch for them.

> **Note**: Your word processor tries to suppress widows and orphans but in doing so might create a large empty space at the bottom of a printed page or column. Space is better than a lonely line on a page.

- When your proof copy arrives, check margins and other spacing. If pages look too tight, negotiate that with your publisher. Generally nonfiction requires more open or white space than fiction, but fiction books with too-narrow margins also look chintzy.
- Assess the placement of sidebars and/or illustrations on the page. Shaded boxes usually look better centered or on the outside edge of a page rather than inside near the gutter.
- Check the frontmatter—all that stuff before the first chapter. You can be adventurous here. Know what rules you are breaking and have a good reason to do so. Know also that e-books have entirely different frontmatter guidelines than paper books. (Find guidelines for formatting books for Kindle in Appendix Six of this book.) If you see something in your proof you don't understand or don't like, ask your publisher. Ditto, if you *don't* see something there you think will help your book or your career.
- Check backmatter, too. A few new ideas won't hurt, especially if yours is a book of nonfiction. Some books and literary journals include

advertising. Remember your high school yearbook? Someone had to pay the bills. It is nice when someone supports the writing community, too.

> **Note:** I like this rundown of what both frontmatter and backmatter consist of and the order in which they might appear at thebookdesigner.com/2009/09/parts-of-a-book/.

- Some publishers use two title pages. The second is called a *half-title page*. Old-timers call them *bastard title pages*. They traditionally appeared before the title page or any other frontmatter. In those days, they were abbreviated versions of the title page that could be torn out before the book was bound. Your publisher may prefer to use two. One defense for the practice is that authors can sign and personalize one page and the book will still have an extra one that is untouched. Another is that an additional title page can separate the book's text from long and complex frontmatter. The setup of a book's frontmatter might be part of your publisher's style guidelines and be nonnegotiable.
- Today many books include one or two pages of blurbs or endorsements just inside the front cover. Don't overdo it. More than two pages is overkill.
- If your book has a contents page, use the term *Contents* as a title. *Table of Contents* is redundant. Don't let your publisher use leaders—those little dots between the chapter's title and

the page number; they are considered archaic or at least unlovely. (See how I did it in this book.)

- Ask your publisher who is responsible for making the index. Today, nonfiction authors whose books are published traditionally are often asked to assemble their own indexes. If the finger points at you, don't get lazy and try to avoid doing it. Anything that will help your reader is worth the time and effort. If you decide to build your own index, expect to spend time reading up on how to do it right; do not rely entirely on the index function of your word processor.

  Note: Consider hiring a professional indexer. The American Society of Indexers (asindexing.org/find-an-indexer/asi-indexer-locator/) is a good place to start a search, and Barbara Wallace at libriservices.com/ offers an e-booklet on indexing for a nominal fee. The *Chicago Manual of Style* (bit.ly/ChiStBk) has an exhaustive chapter on doing your own index.

- Some books include a study guide in the backmatter. Literary novels and some nonfiction books are especially suited to study guides. Consider writing one that illustrates important aspects of your book for teachers or reading groups.
- Those who write textbooks and nonfiction can learn more about formatting headings, subheadings, and even *sub*-subheadings at writing.engr.psu.edu/workbooks/format.html. Alternatively, search Google "formatting

headings" (or any other formatting topic). Try to select tutorials from university Web sites and be sure to determine that the instructions are written for nonfiction and not fiction or vice versa.

- Keep your formatter in the loop from the earliest moment in the publishing process. Adding a single page, paragraph, or even a word can cause havoc for a formatter, so they will appreciate your diligence. The gremlins, of course, love it when you alter something after the formatting is done.

> **Note**: Formatters often use computer programs like PageMaker and InDesign that are very different from Word. Thus, do-it-yourself authors who do not choose to outsource this part of their book's production might face another big learning curve.

- Your author photograph (the one used for your biography) must be professional. If your publisher accepts a snapshot taken by a family member, please reconsider. Professionals do something discernibly different with the pose, the crop, the lighting, and the resolution.
- Use this book to check up on your formatter. Has he or she spaced ellipses correctly? Has he or she rearranged dialogue punctuation from guidelines for books or from your country's preferences (for example, US or UK)? Is his formatting consistent?

After you have done all this, what if the gremlins win a point or two? I will not be the first to throw stones at you or the publisher. I know it is usually the gremlins I should blame. I also know how hard you worked.

Just so you know that I do sympathize, I'm going to have a bumper sticker made. It will say, "I'd rather be writing than matching wits with gremlins."

Congratulations! You are now ready to publish your jewel. Are you going to do it yourself? If you are, please pay special attention to Chapter Seventeen. If you aren't, don't skip it. You may need at least some of the information in it for publishing promotion material or to feel more comfortable partnering with the professionals assigned to you by your publisher.

CHAPTER SEVENTEEN
GOING IT ON YOUR OWN

If you publish your own book—especially if it is your virgin effort—you might run across more than one shocker. Even if you hire an expert team including editors, formatters, cover design artists, public relations people, and a coach, you need to have some notion of how to supervise your chosen experts. There are guidelines and ideas to help you partner with your publisher, printer, and your book cover designer as well as everything you need to market your book (for marketing is indeed an integral part of the concept we call *publishing*!) in my *The Frugal Book Promoter* (bit.ly/FrugalBookPromo). Here are a few pointers, some of them from that book:

- When you hire an artist for your cover, be sure she or he is experienced in book cover design. Ask for samples and compare them with the covers done by the big publishers who have been publishing a long time and (usually) are dead-center-on for producing covers that sell books. Organizations like the Independent Book Publishers Association (IBPA) (ibpa-online.org/) give their members support with any publishing process they encounter (resources, discounts, an excellent forum, a print magazine) and are darn-near essential for those who are going it alone. Chaz DeSimone is the artist who designed the cover for this book (and my original frugal logo and font). He can also help you with your interior design and happens to know a thing or two about copywriting and marketing. Find him at desimonedesign.com/.

- You need to have an idea about what constitutes frontmatter and backmatter and how to put their individual parts in acceptable order. Get ideas from books similar to yours from one of the top New York publishers.
- If you write nonfiction, you should know that someone *else* writes a foreword, usually an expert or celebrity. List their qualifications to clarify their credibility.
- Take a look at that word *foreword*. You need to know how it's spelled.
- You need to know the *preface* is where you— as the author—address your reader.
- If you're a fiction writer and need to write something in the frontmatter to introduce your story, that's probably a *prologue*.

- You need to know little marketing secrets. One of my favorites is making an author's profile page in the AuthorsConnect™ feature of Amazon that serves your readers and establishes *your* credibility. (Amazon is the online bookstore most essential for your book sales.) It includes posts from my blog that talk about things like the content rule I mentioned earlier in this book, about technique, about book promotion, free publicity, about resources, and other things that specifically interest readers of my HowToDoItFrugally books. I also send my Twitter stream to that page. You can see what it looks like by going to bit.ly/CarolynsAmazProfile.

Another favorite is how to get reviews from major review journals even if you've missed their deadlines. I discuss both in my *The Frugal Book Promoter* and will cover the latter in more depth in my coming book, *Your Frugal Book Reviews: Getting Credible Reviews the Old-Fashioned Way Without Paying for Them* (working title).

Note: My most frugal suggestion for self-publishers—and the one most likely to keep your book on the track to success—is to avoid larger subsidy-publishers that are identifiable as what some call vanity presses. Unfortunately, prejudice surrounding the press a book is published on still

SIDEBAR
Heart Attacks Can Be Avoided

Subsidy- and self-publishers beware! When I received galleys for my first book, a novel, I was shocked at the blank pages scattered throughout. This wasn't a self-published book, but if it had been, I would have been even more appalled. I had no one to nudge me out of my stupor. You would have been amused at my collecting blank pages, noting the page numbers on them (or the numbers that would have been on them if any had appeared).

Knowing that blank pages are a natural function because all chapters begin on right-hand, odd-numbered pages (even if that means the one across from it on the left goes stitch naked) would have kept me from having a mini heart attack.

##

exists, though it is steadily diminishing. The best way to avoid book bigotry is to produce a professional book. If you are going it on your own, hire help when you need it and use a press name of your own choosing. If you decide to partner with a book shepherd or press that is a lovely mix of subsidy- and traditional publishing, choose one with a name that doesn't stand up and shout "self-published." If you prefer a larger subsidy press, negotiate an imprint of your own. The latter is a longshot, but it might work.

This is only a brief rundown on formatting and interior structure. I include it because one small aspect of publishing like formatting can be an indicator of your professionalism and because the more you know about this business we are in (we authors are smack-dab in the publishing business whether or not we like to think of it that way), the better equipped you will be to avoid booboos. When your publishing process goes astray—whether it's the fault of your traditional publishing house, those you hire, or the errors are on your own shoulders, *you* are the one wh suffers.

YOUR PUBLISHING EDUCATION WEB-STYLE

If you use the Web to educate yourself about publishing and editing, consider the credibility of the authors and/or the site you are using. When in doubt, utilize the ones associated with universities.

- Subscribe to the *Chicago Manual of Style* online for a yearly fee. If you buy the real book, you won't have to divvy up for a information every time you have a question in the years after you publish your first book. You won't, of course, get updates with the paper edition. Here's the URL: chicagomanualofstyle.org/subscription_opts.html.

- Gorham Printing offers a free e-book (gorhamprinting.com/home-book-printer/catalog.php) that includes lots of helpful information on publishing.
- Of course, you will find recommended books—paper or online—for further study in Appendix Two of this book and more extensive help on my Web site (howtodoitfrugally.com/links_for_writers.htm) where you'll find articles, tips, and rarely seen lists of things like media-release disseminators, accessible contests, and US universities' Masters of Fine Arts in writing programs.

Drum roll please! Let's celebrate. You are ready to send your work out to be scrutinized by the publishing world. Yay!

But don't let your guard down. Keep your professional writer's hat on. The publishing industry is traditional—even if you're self-published. So, put your best book forward. Follow the rules in this book for whatever you send out like query letters, media releases, cover letters and even e-mail!

CHAPTER EIGHTEEN
PUTTING YOUR WORK
OUT INTO THE WORLD

You believe you have done all you can to flush out the gremlins and keep their three-toed tracks from appearing anywhere in your presentation. It is time to put your spotless letter, proposal, submission, or galleys into an envelope and post or send the package digitally to one or more of those gatekeepers.

The mailing process should be easy, but even it is rigged with traps for the unwary. Entire movies have been built around the premise of mail that gets dropped into a postbox just before the poor shmuck thinks of one last thing he should have said or a mistake he made. Postal workers don't return mistakes because you want them to, and unless you trace online submissions, you might not know if yours got lost in cyberspace.

Note: If you are starting your writing career, you might be surprised at how many publishers, agents, and especially literary journals still specify hardcopy submissions only.

My husband, author of *What Foreigners Need To Know About America From A To Z* (amzn.to/ForeignersAmericaUS), once bought some extra-sturdy mailers for his manuscript because it was heavier and fatter than most (you'd be surprised how much immigrants, international students, and business people the world over need to know about America and how to work or play with Americans). He didn't want his work to accidentally get spread all over an agent's office, papers flying everywhere. This considerate gesture so annoyed one agent that he sent an e-mail lamenting how hard it had been to open the package (try scissors!) and how he had just tossed it into his wastebasket. So much for trying to please all the people all of the time, but it also serves as a reminder to never deviate from the guidelines.

Another editor I interviewed for this book hates it when an eleven-page short story gets stuffed into a regular letter-size envelope instead of a large, flat manila envelope or mailer provided by FedEx or the US postal service. I assume that is because an envelope that looks like an overstuffed kielbasa does not make a professional presentation. So the magic words are *clean, clear, no frills, no folding.* Follow submission suggestions. Do not deviate.

I have been told that *The Frugal Book Promoter* is so full of specific, practical information it is impossible to digest. After you get the big picture by reading the whole of that book (or this one) and apply the ideas that you are in immediate need of, think of these books as references and use the indexes every time you face a new project. Both books are designed to help you find every entry on a particular subject or process you are dealing with at any given moment. Even my e-books have lists of topics (without page numbers because, as you know, e-books page numbers are slippery little devils). These research aids are there so that you don't need to develop a photographic memory. You might even find entries on subjects that you forgot I covered. Go back. Reread. Use the great references and resources I have given you. Together we can be a real force for professional submissions and a mighty challenge to gremlins everywhere.

WHEN MAIL IS YOUR FIRST FOOT IN THE DOOR

Here are a few guidelines to help get your manuscript off in style by USPS (United States Postal Service) or other services when gatekeepers' guidelines express a preference for hardcopies.

- Buy new envelopes that fit your unfolded manuscript. You may use letter-sized envelopes for submitting small works like poetry to contests.
- Use manuscript mailing boxes when an agent or publisher requests a hardcopy of a hefty manuscript. Smaller manuscripts may be paperclipped at the upper left corner, but do not use staples.
- Include SASE (Self-Addressed Stamped Envelope) for replies—or enough in postage to get your manuscript back to you in the same box you sent. Do this even when SASEs are not mentioned in the guidelines. It is the mark of a professional. This goes for anything you want returned or want a yea or nay answer for—from a short story or poem for a contest to a manuscript to an agent.
- If your computer skills are up to it, print professional address labels. If they aren't, use

commercial address labels, print neatly, and be accurate with both name and address. USPS supplies sturdy preprinted envelopes for priority and express mail—envelopes that look professional even if you handwrite the address.

- Don't do anything cute on the envelope. Only "Requested Material" is allowed and only if the material has truly been requested.

- Most of the agents who responded to my call for suggestions for this book are adamant about following their submission guidelines and just as intense about checking to be sure all the required parts of your submission are enclosed. Do not assume that once you have mastered the process for one agent, you don't need to check the requirements for another.

- Always include a cover letter. Even a short cover letter. Even if it isn't required. Even if you already sent a query letter and your communication is expected. A cover letter on quality letterhead stationery marks you as a professional. A human being is on the other end of every letter or e-mail you send. I cannot tell you how many submissions I get for my review blog (thenewbookreview.blogspot.com/) or my newsletter (howtodoitfrugally.com/newsletter_&_blog.htm) that don't let me know which of my services they need, let alone include a greeting.

- If you are mailing overseas and want an answer or your materials returned, enclose an IRC (International Reply Coupon) with your cover letter. Your post office personnel can help you with this process.

- Apply accurate postage. Returns for postage cost money, waste time (you could miss a deadline), and leave your envelope looking grungy. If that should happen, pop for a clean envelope.

WHEN E-MAIL IS PREFERRED

We have talked about professionalism, but e-mails seem to encourage sloppy, impersonal, too personal, or just plain inconsiderate behavior. I'm guilty of a bit of sloppiness in e-mails going to friends. When you send an e-mail to gatekeepers or business associates, you are being judged. I feel compelled to remind you to avoid anything too funsie. That is not to say you can't let your personality shine though. You should. But no smiling faces, multiple exclamation points, or fancy backgrounds that make your e-mail hard to read. Review the chapters and entries in this book on query and cover letters, especially the one that lists agents' pet peeves.

Here are guidelines for sending your submission packages by e-mail when guidelines tell you it is preferred. (Notice this doesn't say when *you* prefer it.)

- If you want your e-mail read, your powerful subject line will help make that happen:
  - Clearly define what you are sending, query letter, requested submission, paid submission, or contest. Or follow the agent or publisher's guidelines.
  - It is OK—even desirable—to follow this essential information with an intriguing headline that makes your contact want to know more: "Query Letter: Feature Idea

Based on Your Recent Rant on Immigration"

- Do not try to mislead your contact with the subject line to get them to open it. Do try to make it so clear they will know it is not spam. "Hello" will surely make them think someone is trying to "fool Mother Nature."

- The e-mail window where you type your text becomes your cover letter. It includes:

  - A greeting, preferably using your contact's name, correctly spelled.

  - A mention that the material requested is attached or available. Tell your contact exactly what is attached. It doesn't hurt to add something like "in accordance with the guidelines on your Web site."

> **Caution**: Do not attach anything to your e-mail unless expressly invited to do so in guidelines provided by your contact. To avoid viruses, many services and organizations block or will not open an e-mail with attachments so when you get no response, you may believe you are being ignored. If you find no guidelines regarding attachments, ask your contact how they prefer you send your manuscript.

- A thank you for consideration or opportunity.
- Your signature. E-mail signatures are very important. Most e-mail services allow you to design a signature that goes out automatically with each e-mail. For contact with fellow professionals, it includes your full home, business, or PO Box address; phone or cell number or both; and fax number. Your e-mails to the media, agents, and publishers are not the time to worry about privacy. Supplying complete information is a courtesy that saves them (and you) time.
- It is nice to include in your e-mail a notice similar to the "enc." (enclosure) designation left over from typewriter days when it alerted recipients to enclosures in snail mail. You can update it to "See four files attached" or "See the paste below my e-signature."
- If the file for your manuscript is too big or unacceptable as an attachment, use a search engine to find a service that can accommodate it. Or zip the file. Or use a shared link from the cloud. A .pdf file is acceptable for some agents and publishers, but not all.

Now, sit back satisfied that your manuscript package is on its way. Celebrate that your submission will be judged professional because it is well edited and other aspects of your presentation indicate that you are aware of the expectations and traditions of the publishing industry.

Though there are many aspects of your marketing campaign you should have been working on during the time you were writing and editing, it is now time to learn the intricacies of media (press) releases, media kits, working with the media folks who can help expose your book to readers—people like bloggers, feature and business editors, and radio and TV hosts and producers.

Read the second edition of *The Frugal Book Promoter* (bit.ly/FrugalBookPromo) or one of the other books on book marketing listed in Appendix Two of this book. I always say, "Reading one good book on marketing your book is never enough." I also say, "Great editing *is* marketing!" It's a major part of how you present yourself.

Now is *your* time to shine. Good job.

APPENDICES

APPENDIX ONE
EDITING AT A GLANCE

Of course the title of this Appendix is hype. "At a glance," indeed! You know by now that editing is a craft all its own. I do want to make the process as easy as possible for you, so here is a brief checklist to review once you are sure you are ready:

- Organize your desktops—both your computer's and the for-real one.
- Order presentation materials so they will be ready when your editing is done. You will not want your newly edited material idling away while you get stationery printed. *The Frugal Book Promoter* explains the necessity of beginning your branding efforts and the review-gathering process early because it is so essential to the health of your book.
- Set up your e-mail presentation including your autosignature so your e-mail contacts have everything they need at their fingertips. It's the professional thing to do. It's professional because it's considerate. Before your book is published, that signature can work as prepromotion. After it is published, it becomes an essential part of your marketing campaign.
- Your hardcopy edit comes first.
- Your computer edit—the automated one—comes next.
- Now you do more manual edits including cleaning up extra spaces in your copy.

- Now comes edits and critiques from your detail-oriented pal, your typical-reader buddy, and your fellow experts.
- You have been using your spelling checker, but this is a good time to repeat the process. Remember it is only a friend when you treat it with utmost caution.
- Only now will those of you who are committed to do-it-yourself editing have a real take on whether or not you need to hire an editor.
- Do your galley or proof-copy edit. A full edit is warranted after any formatting adjustment or automated computer change.
- Check up on your formatter who uses touchy programs other than Word and, because she is a professional, will want your extra pair of eyes.
- Check this checklist. During the Ebola crisis, you may have read how important checklists are to pilots and infectious disease specialists. They work for writers, too.
- Recheck submission guidelines of any agent, publisher, or contest director you are contacting before you send your packet by snail mail or e-mail.
- Mail or e-mail your manuscript package to the publisher or agent and celebrate!
- Repeat as needed.

Note: Online magic has provided us with a way to submit manuscripts using forms found on your contact's Web site. They may include ways to pay with your credit card or Paypal when fees are involved. Most are secure sites.

APPENDIX TWO
RECOMMENDED READING AND RESOURCES

This is a list of resources and references I like. I mentioned some earlier in this book and add a few more here for readers who find the editing process as addictive as chewing gum. There are also some to help you with other aspects of the publishing process.

EDITING

- *Lapsing Into a Coma: A Curmudgeon's Guide to the Many Things That Can Go Wrong in Print—And How to Avoid Them* by Bill Walsh (bit.ly/LapsingComa).
- Concordance is a text-analyzing computer program that makes indexes and wordlists, counts word frequency, compares uses of a word, analyzes keywords, finds phrases and idioms, and publishes to the Web: concordancesoftware.co.uk/.
- Writing Help is a collection of computer programs by Roger Carlson, including highlighters for passive words, prepositions, and adverbs as well as an "Adverb Eliminator," "Word Frequency Counter," and "Count Lines." You need some computer expertise to set your computer's security settings to accept macros, reboot your computer so the new settings will take effect, and install the programs. For more, go to rogerjcarlson.com/WritingHelp/TechTips.html.

EDITORS

- Barbara McNichol, editor and writer (barbaramcnichol.com/), was introduced earlier in this book. Nonfiction only.
- Virgil Jose, freelance editor for nonfiction, may be reached at gilrod2007@yahoo.com.
- For an editor with a UK sensibility (though he edits for Yanks, too, including this one), check Dr. Bob Rich, robert.rich01@bigpond.com.
- Yvonne Perry, owner of Writers in the Sky (writersinthesky.com/), is a developmental editor for fiction and nonfiction. She also has team members who copyedit.
- Robin Quinn (writingandediting.biz) provides all aspects of editing from developmental consulting and manuscript evaluations, to proofreading services. Reach her at quinnwordforword@aol.com or 310-838-7098.

GRAMMAR AND STYLE

- *AP Stylebook* by Associated Press (bit.ly/AssocPressStyle). Especially good for those who write for newspapers and some magazines.
- *Bryson's Dictionary of Troublesome Words: A Writer's Guide to Getting It Right* by Bill Bryson (bit.ly/Brysons).
- *Chicago Manual of Style* by the University of Chicago Press Staff (bit.ly/ChiStBk).
- *Eats, Shoots & Leaves: The Zero Tolerance Approach to Punctuation* by Lynne Truss (http://bit.ly/ShootsLeaves). Especially good (and fun) for those writing for the UK market.
- *Far From the Madding Gerund* by Geoffrey K. Pullum et al (bit.ly/MaddingGerund).
- *Garner's Modern American Usage* by Bryan A. Garner (bit.ly/USAUsage) is excellent for Americans.

For our purposes—that is not to rile an agent or publisher—choose the more formal of possibilities it offers. If the suggestion feels stilted, rearrange the construction of your sentence.

- *Grammar Snobs Are Big Meanies: Guide to Language for Fun & Spite* by June Casagrande (bit.ly/GrammarSnobs), published by Penguin. Use this book when you want to be informed and confident enough to edit on your own or to judge the expertise of the editor you hire. It is an excellent source (and a fun one) to learn more about style choice vs. grammar rules. A more formal tome that helps with basics but isn't as fun is *The New Fowler's Modern English Usage* by Fowler and Burchfield (bit.ly/FowlersUsage).
- *Mortal Syntax: 101 Language Choices That Will Get You Clobbered by the Grammar Snobs—Even If You're Right* by June Casagrande (bit.ly/MortalSyntax). The more you know about choices, the better writer you'll be. You will not always need to cater to gatekeepers.
- *It Was the Best of Sentences, It Was the Worst of Sentences: A Writer's Guide to Crafting Killer Sentences* by June Casagrande (bit.ly/BestSentences). This is the best single book to review before you begin to edit any major writing project.
- *StyleEase for Chicago Manual of Style* by Kate Turabian (http://bit.ly/ChicagoHelp).
- *A Manual for Writers of Research Papers, Theses, and Dissertations, Seventh Edition: Chicago Style for Students and Researchers* by Kate L. Turabian (bit.ly/ChicagoHelp) is an excellent resource for academics.
- *Perrin and Smith Handbook of Current English* has been around a long time. When you have read it, you will know the difference between temerity and

timidity—or at least know to look them up. "Half knowing a word may be more dangerous than not knowing it at all" is the kind of truth you will find within its pages. Trouble is, you may need to search for it in a bookstore that sells used books or watch for it at garage sales.

- *The Elements of Style,* Fourth Edition, by William Strunk Jr., E. B. White, Roger Angell (bit.ly/ElementsStyle). See my cautionary notes in this book about using *Elements* as if it were The Ten Commandments.

- *The Describer's Dictionary: A Treasury of Terms & Literary Quotations* by David Grambs (bit.ly/Describers). One of my favorite references for creative writing.

- *When Words Collide: A Media Writer's Guide to Grammar and Style* (Wadsworth Series in Mass Communication and Journalism) by Lauren Kessler and Duncan McDonald (bit.ly/WordsCollide). Perfect for freelance writers, copywriters, journalists, and media writers.

WRITING CRAFT

- *Writing Dialogue* by Tom Chiarella (bit.ly/Chiarella) is a must-read because poor dialogue technique is a glaring tipoff to editors and publishers that a manuscript is written by a beginner who has not taken the time to learn his or her craft. It is one of those books I wish I had written myself. No need. Chiarella did it.

- *Writing for Emotional Impact: Advanced Dramatic Techniques to Attract, Engage, and Fascinate the Reader from Beginning to End* by Karl Iglesias (bit.ly/KarlIglesias). Fiction writers can learn a lot from screenwriters and playwrights and vice versa.

- *Wired for Story* by Lisa Cron (bit.ly/WiredStory). I recommend this book to all my editing clients.
- *How to Blog a Book: Write, Publish, and Promote Your Work One Post at a Time* by Nina Amir (bit.ly/BlogABook). A Writer's Digest book that encourages and inspires—and makes the writing of your book a little easier.

CUSTOM DICTIONARIES

Many professional organizations share their print conventions with authors. Just ask. I list a few so you will see there might be an appropriate one for you even if your topic is . . . well . . . esoteric.

- Zoologists and those who write about wildlife and other science-oriented topics will find free custom dictionaries at home.comcast.net/~wildlifebio/c_dic.htm.
- Here is a custom dictionary for medical terms: ptcentral.com/university/medterms_zip.html.
- Find a tree and woody plant dictionary at shade-trees.tripod.com/tree_dic.html.

PUBLISHING, PROMOTION, AND MARKETING

- *Talk Radio Wants You: An Intimate Guide to 700 Shows and How to Get Invited* by Francine Silverman (bit.ly/TalkShowResources). She also has a reasonably priced radio referral service.
- *Making the Perfect Pitch: How to Catch a Literary Agent's Eye* by Katherine Sands (bit.ly/YourPerfectPitch). Straight from the mouth of a literary agent.
- *The Frugal Book Promoter: How to get nearly free publicity on your own or by partnering with your publisher*, Second Edition by Carolyn Howard-Johnson (bit.ly/FrugalBookPromo).
- *The ABCs of POD: A Beginner's Guide to Fee-Based Print-on-Demand Publishing* by Dehanna Bailee

(bit.ly/ABDPublishing). This book provides basics for those considering self- or subsidy-publishing.

- *The Complete Guide to Self-Publishing: Everything You Need to Know to Write, Publish, Promote and Sell Your Own Book* by Marilyn Ross (bit.ly/MarilynRoss).
- *The Well-Fed Self-Publisher* by Peter Bowerman (wellfedsp.com). Includes marketing because *to publish* includes *to market.*
- *How to Publish and Promote Your Book Now* by L. Diane Wolfe (bit.ly/HowToPub). Diane boils down what you need to know to essentials.

BOOK PROPOSALS
- *The Great First Impression Book Proposal: Everything You Need to Know About Selling Your Book to an Agent or Publisher in Thirty Minutes or Less* by Carolyn Howard-Johnson (bit.ly/BookProposals). A booklet. Available in paperback and as an e-book.
- *Book Proposals That Sell, 21 Secrets to Speed Your Success* by Terry Whalin (bit.ly/TerryWhalin).
- *How to Write a Book Proposal* by agent Michael Larsen (bit.ly/MichaelLarsen).

TYPESETTING AND/OR FORMATTING
- *From Word to Kindle: Self Publishing Your Kindle Book with Microsoft Word, or Tips for Designing and Formatting Your Text So Your Ebook Doesn't Look Horrible (Like Everyone Else's).* It's very frugal at ninety-nine cents. By Aaron Shephard (bit.ly/Formatting4Kindle). E-book only.
- *Stop Stealing Sheep and Find Out How Type Works*, Third Edition by Erik Spiekermann (bit.ly/HowToTypeSet).
- *The Complete Manual of Typography: A Guide to Setting Perfect Type*, Second Edition, by Jim Felici (bit.ly/TypographyGuide).

HAVING FUN
Sun Signs for Writers (Writer's Digest) by Bev
Walton-Porter. Kindle edition
(bit.ly/SunSignsWriters).

DIRECTORIES: MARKETPLACES FOR YOUR WORK
There are many directories, but I like *Writer's Market*, published by Writer's Digest Books (bit.ly/WritersMarkets). Most writers use this general directory because it accommodates all genres, but Writer's Digest publishes smaller ones targeted for markets like poetry, novels, short stories, Christian markets, and children's markets. Everyone uses them. You might have the mistaken idea that its popularity is a disadvantage because so many people have access to the listed resources, but they vet their entries, they are coded so you find what you want—even contests—and they keep all their directories current.

APPENDIX THREE

I recommend these agents because they cared enough to offer their time to make the query process better for you. Obviously, they haven't all been my agents. Each author (and each agent) has an individual personality. Each author (and each agent) has a specific product range to sell. Whether you are a match for any one of them is strictly up to you (and to them). I am not listing their e-mail addresses. I want you (and they want you) to go to their Web sites to learn who they are, what they do and, most of all, what their submission guidelines are. Their e-mail addresses or contact info are there, too.

- Laurie Abkemeier, DeFiore and Company (defioreandco.com/).
- Jenoyne Adams, now an author.
- Jenny Bent, The Bent Agency, New York/London (thebentagency.com/contact.php).
- Roberta Brown, Brown Literary Agency (brownliteraryagency.com/).
- Scott Eagan, Greyhaus Literary Agency (greyhausagency.com/).
- Lisa Ekus-Saffer, The Lisa Ekus Group (lisaekus.com/).
- Elaine P. English, PLLC Literary (elaineenglish.com/). Literary agent and attorney.
- Lilly Ghahremani, a founding member of Full Circle Literary (fullcircleliterary.com/).
- Michael Larsen and Elizabeth Pomada, Michael Larsen–Elizabeth Pomada Literary (larsenpomada.com/).

- Tamela Hancock Murray, Steve Laube Agency (stevelaube.com/).
- Kristin Nelson, Nelson Literary Agency, LLC (nelsonagency.com/).
- Gina Panettieri, Talcott Notch Literary (talcottnotch.net/).
- Stephanie Kip Rostan, Levine/Greenberg Literary (levinegreenberg.com/).
- Kae Tienstra, KT Public Relations & Literary Services (ktpublicrelations.com/contact/).
- Liz Trupin-Pulli, Jet Literary (jetliterary.com/).
- Matt Wagner, Fresh Books Literary Agency (fresh-books.com/).
- Terrie Wolf, AKA Literary (akaliteraryllc.com/).
- Michelle Wolfson, Wolfson Literary (wolfsonliterary.com/).

> **Note**: I do not ascribe to the idea that the only powerful agents have offices in New York or agents can only *be* powerful if they have offices in New York. This is the age of computers and e-books after all.

APPENDIX FOUR
SAMPLE COVER LETTER

A cover letter is very similar to a query letter except that it introduces a media kit or some other marketing material or enclosure like a manuscript requested by an agent. A query asks for something specific, like representation or media coverage. (See Appendix Five for samples of queries.)

If you know or have spoken to whomever you are contacting, your cover letter may be friendly and, depending on your personal style, you may use a first name. If this is a first contact, use the person's proper title (Mr., Mrs., Ms., Miss), but avoid stiff formality unless you perceive an overwhelming reason to do so. A cover letter uses the Times New Roman font (12 point). It is single-spaced and one page only.

Notice that the sample cover letter below includes an invitation to an event near the end of the letter. It is polite and smart marketing to invite the media to be part of your plans. Find more information on what to include and avoid in Chapter Five "Dangerous Corners Ahead: Covers and Queries."

These two examples of cover letters and all but one of the examples of query letters I include in Appendix Five are for fiction rather than nonfiction. Generally speaking, it is easier for authors to find the right information and tone to sell and promote nonfiction. Fiction writers often need a little extra guidance, but ideas from all the examples can be applied to both fiction and nonfiction.

SAMPLE COVER LETTER FOR A MEDIA KIT

As you can see, this cover letter also serves as a query letter because it tells the contact exactly what the author is hoping might come from the communication.

[A professional letterhead goes here or that information becomes part of your signature if you use e-mail.]
Date: xxx

Contact's name, e-mail, Web site address, and street address or post office box address.

Dear Marilee,

It has been a while since we spoke about your reviewing my book, *This Is the Place*. As you can see, it is a bit late, but July 1st is now AmErica House's release date. Since we spoke, *This Is the Place* won Sime-Gen.com's Reviewers' Choice Award in their mainstream category. Nominations are made by reviewers nationwide. I hope you can find a spot for an interview in your busy radio schedule.

I am a journalist who got lost for about forty years. I conceived an idea for a novel when I was writing for my high school newspaper; it gestated through my years as a staff writer at *The Salt Lake Tribune*, and *Good Housekeeping*, my years as a publicist, and for about four decades doing various things that kept me from writing..

Many, including the editors at the *Los Angeles Daily News*, have found my writing a book at an age when most are considering retirement an interesting news angle. At the age of sixty-two I found a publisher, several of my short stories placed in the finals of national literary contests, I completed my first screenplay, and I started to study writing again at UCLA and several universities in Europe.

That *This Is the Place* tells the stories of four generations of Utah women, from the 1800s to the 1950s, interests western history buffs and those who like women's literature. Its premise is that intolerance can be corrosive even when it is cloaked in family, love, religion, and community.

This Is the Place's release date coincides with the burgeoning interest in Utah as the 2002 Winter Olympics approach.

I am enclosing a media kit and an unedited review copy of my novel (with a generic cover). If there is anything else I can do for you, please let me know. I have headshots, a jpeg file of my book cover and other assorted promotional materials you might need. My first official reading and signing will be at Vroman's on Thursday, July 26, at 7 p.m. and I would love to see you there.

Thank you for your consideration.

Sincerely,
Carolyn Howard-Johnson
Encs: 2

SAMPLE COVER LETTER FOR SUBMISSIONS TO JOURNALS, CONTESTS

These days cover letters are mostly sent by e-mail or pasted into the window of a form on a review journal's Web site. A pitch or query must *sell* the idea of a piece rather than merely presenting the story, poem, or other enclosure. An editor at the respected literary journal *Glimmer Train* says, "The cover letter needs to be simple, polite, and friendly. Mention any previous publications, but don't worry if you have none." Here is a sample.

Dear Mr. or Ms. Editor's Name,

Thank you for the opportunity to submit my story to your literary journal [or contest].[Use the specific title.]

I recently picked up my first copy of *Glimmer Train* and enjoyed the stories, especially "My Friend's Foe" by XXXX. I would be honored to see my story "The Rye Maker's Daughter" in your fall issue. [Don't fake this. Say what you mean, what is true. You should be reading—at least occasionally—the journals you submit to.]

My work has appeared in an online journal called *Long Story Short* and I write a column for my community college's weekly newspaper.

I hope you enjoy the read.

Sincerely,

XXXX
See attached [Attach only if the journal's Web site or rules give you permission to do so. Otherwise, follow their guidelines.]

APPENDIX FIVE

SAMPLE QUERY LETTERS

I include several different kinds of query letters as samples for you to follow in this Appendix. Unfortunately, there is no way to provide templates for each of the many possible reasons an author might need to send a query letter, including requests for representation, for a publisher, for an interview with a blogger or podcaster, for a feature story with a newspaper. The list is endless. These samples can only serve as general templates because each title is different and each request is different, but if you follow the suggestions for query letters I gave you earlier in this book and use these samples for ideas, you can't go wrong.

SAMPLE QUERY LETTER FOR FILM CONSIDERATION FOR A WORK OF FICTION

I wish I could tell you that this query letter was successful, that *This Is the Place* had been optioned for a film featuring vistas of the craggy Wasatch Mountains in Utah. Mr. Redford's office returned my book. It looked as if it had not been opened and was accompanied by a note that appeared personal (signed by Redford's secretary). She advised that accepting books over the transom (transom is publishing talk for material sent without an invitation or benefit of an agent) was fraught with legal problems. I had learned—even after years of experience as a publicist—how our litigious culture affects writers. It was one of the potholes I fell into and is an example of the experiences

I love to pass along to my readers so they will benefit from my mistakes. Still, this letter illustrates that the best letters are personalized in whatever way you can find.

If this query strikes you as a longshot, it is. I urge you to go against the odds. If you think your book has the right stuff, shoot for the stars. However, don't aim for stars that aren't in the same galaxy as your book. You do not have the time to waste asking people to do something that is outside their expertise or genre. I chose Robert Redford because we had remote Utah connections and because the literary quality of my books and his films seem to be a match.

[A professional letterhead goes here or that information becomes part of your signature if you use e-mail.]

Date
Mr. Robert Redford
South Fork Pictures
xxxxx
xxxxxx

Dear Mr. Redford,

When I was a little girl, I lived next door to the VanWagenens [relatives of Redford's wife] in Provo. Later I moved to Salt Lake City to begin my writing career at *The Salt Lake Tribune*. When my husband graduated from the U [University of Utah], we moved to New York where he attended graduate school and I worked as a fashion publicist. Later, my husband worked with Richard [Mr. Redford's relative] at a consulting firm in Los Angeles. It is a small world.

I wrote a book several years ago titled *This Is the Place* because it was a story that had to be told. It has won numerous awards and I am now exploring options for a movie. Because of your interest in the West and the literary tone of your work, you are the first person I have contacted.

Set in Utah in the 1950s (about the time you and I were growing up), *This Is the Place* is a semi-biographical novel dealing with the pain and ecstasy of overcoming religious intolerance. My lead character and I are of Mormon heritage but not LDS; we are both women who followed our hearts in times when women had few choices. *This Is the Place* recounts our struggles and some of my Mormon family's pioneer stories. I overcame the effects of intolerance; my Protestant mother never did.

My main character overcomes it, too. The book is a story about her journey.

Although I feel that my portrayal of Utah's beauty is part of its strength, a screenplay could very easily deal with Jewish vs. non-Jewish, black vs. white, Asian vs. non-Asian because intolerance is so . . . well, generic. The tone of the movie *Bend It Like Beckham* reminded me of *This Is the Place*, and my character and I both relate to the angst Julianne Moore portrayed in the 1950s setting of *Far From Heaven*.

I have enclosed a copy of *This Is the Place* with another book of mine that was recently published titled *Harkening*. One of the stories in it was based on an experience I had with the VanWagenen mother (I was only about six—I don't remember her first name—you will recognize her, I'm sure) under the title "Neighbors." You might also enjoy one set in Springville titled "Summerville" and "Helper," a story about my father's and my adventures when he took me with him to deliver Cokes in Helper, Utah. I am enclosing copies from the review journal in which it recently appeared.

I wish you continued success and hope to hear from you.

Sincerely,
Carolyn Howard-Johnson
Encs.

SAMPLE QUERY LETTER FOR A PUBLISHER FOR NONFICTION

The book discussed in this query letter is now published in English under the title *What Foreigners Need To Know About America From A To Z* (amzn.to/ForeignersAmericaUS) with permission of the author and is a recommended text for visiting Fulbright scholars. Because of the author's efforts, this book is now also being translated to Ukrainian and published there at a time when that country wants to become more closely associated with the West. Persistence in pursuing our careers counts!

[A professional letterhead goes here or that information becomes part of your signature if you use e-mail.]

Dear [US Publisher],

Oriental Press, Beijing, China's largest publisher, recently published my *What Asians Need to Know About America, From A to Z.* The book's ISBN is 7-5060-2464-0. Oriental purchased the worldwide Chinese language rights twelve months into my two-year writing effort and it quickly sold through the advance and is poised to pay royalties soon. The book has received strong endorsement, including those of Singapore ambassadors to the UN and the U.S. and Chinese ambassadors from China to the U.S. and U.S. to China.

I wrote *A to Z* for people in China *and* for the millions of Chinese in the U.S. who are baffled by our culture and language. There is no place outside China where those interested in learning more about America, its people and culture can access my book and it is not yet available in English though many professors in China have told me they would prefer to teach students in their American Studies programs with an English edition. Though there is nothing else like it in the United States, there is a serious need for it. Reading the book is like taking an America 101 course. I distill this very broad subject into a neat, well organized, fun, and easy-to-understand package.

The U.S. has millions of Chinese Americans, and more than 200,000 Chinese students study here each year, each of whom would benefit from *A to Z.* Because our relations with China are expanding, increasing numbers of Chinese managers are relocating to the US. In short, the U.S. market for the book is gigantic, just as it is in China.

I am helping Oriental find an importer/distributor for the US. The Book Export/Import Company in China is handling the book there. You may contact Mr. Yang at Oriental Press for more information at xxxx@xxxx.xxx.

I can send PDF files by attachment if you wish. They would include the book's introductory pages (from the English manuscript) including the Contents, as well as pictures of the book's front and back covers. If you would like me to send you a complimentary book for your review, please let me know.

Thank you for your assistance. Please let me know if you have any questions.

Best wishes,
Lance Johnson
Author of *What Asians Need to Know About America, From A to Z*

SAMPLE QUERY LETTER FOR AN AGENT— FICTION

This letter is an example of how humor and letting your personality shine through can be a plus. Those qualities let authors with few or no publishing credits make their voices heard. (Notice how the author uses his education and his college writing experience to his advantage even though he has no creative writing credits.) This young author begins his letter with a quote from his book to give the agent an idea of the voice in his novel.

[A professional letterhead goes here for a query sent by post. For e-mail, include complete information in the e-mail signature.]

Date

Dear Agent: [Use the agent's name, correctly spelled of course!]

Jimmy stands in the doorway with a flask in one hand and a cigarette in the other. He surveys the room until he commands the attention of every customer in the joint. He's wearing a suit and tie and his black hair glistens beneath the pale lights. Slowly he strolls into the club. The volume of the room diminishes. He sits at the piano bench. He clears his throat. He rests his cigarette on top of the piano and the smoke twists upward in tight loops before the stream widens and fades off like a paintbrush being dragged across the canvas as it runs out of paint. His fingers begin tinkling the keys. His eyes are shut. His head sways to the tempo of the tune he's playing. No one in the room clinks a fork or whispers a word.

The Devil's Whipping His Wife is a literary novel set almost entirely in early World War II Los Angeles. It is a nostalgic, character-driven story written in third person but, as you can see by the paragraph above in italics, switches to present tense to spotlight critical scenes, particularly where the literal spotlight is on the protagonist. The story centers around four young adults, but particularly that of Jimmy Portside and his unorthodox rise to fame as a brilliant entertainer, his exploits, and his inevitable fall. Tolerance, hubris, abuse, friendship, and nonconformity are themes that have probably been around in books and stories since before the invention of the wheel.

The Devil's Whipping His Wife is my first completed novel. I'm thirty-two years old and have a BFA degree in theater and a minor in creative writing at UC Santa Barbara. I was a staff writer for the Ventura College Newspaper and had my own column. I've also studied privately with several authors associated with California universities. I'm now working as a beekeeper to finance my need to write.

Thus far, my sole accomplishment has been a lifelong member of the American general public. As a child, I believed Bugs Bunny cartoons represented real life, and as a result stabbed a neighbor's dog with a small piece of mining equipment. I hope to hear from you soon.

David Reel,
Author (Permission to republish granted by author.)

APPENDIX SIX
FORMATTING FOR KINDLE MADE EASY

Though Kindle's program for uploading an e-book is constantly changing and Amazon continues to make conversion easier, I think my beginning-to-end formatting instructions will be useful well into the future and might be helpful for formatting books for other e-readers as well.

> **Note**: Contrary to what many believe, your readers can buy an e-book that can be read most any place including on their computer from Kindle. After they have purchased your e-book, they will be offered a free app and given a choice of the format they want their e-book delivered in. If the process doesn't meet their expectations, they can cancel their order using Amazon's user-friendly account link.

Formatting e-books feels more intuitive if we remember that the pages change every time a reader changes the size of a font and they do that often.

- Start with your fully edited manuscript in Word.
- Save your copy as a doc., *not* .docx, or .rtf (rich text format).
- Use a simple font, preferably Times New Roman or Verdana. Eleven point works nicely for e-readers because the font size can be self-adjusted if readers want it larger.
- Do not use bullets, at least not fancy ones. Here is what the Kindle folks say: "Please know, basic

(black dot) bullet points will reflect well on KDP [Kindle Digital] conversion. However, please avoid using fancy bullet points or numbered bullets. Fancy bullet points do not convert well."

- Single space your text.
- Use one-inch margins all the way around.
- If your book is fiction, change the paragraph indent from .5 to .2 inches. If you write nonfiction, don't indent at all. Put spaces between your paragraphs instead.
- Remove any headers or footers from your copy. That includes text of any sort and page numbers. Don't mistake headers and footers for headings, subheadings, etc. Leave your headings and subheadings in your copy, though you might want to simplify them.
- Set justification. That is the little section in the Word ribbon at the top of your screen that lets you move text all to the left, all to the right, center it, or **justify** it on both right and left. Most suggest you use the latter so the copy looks even on both sides.
- If you want to use live links in the body of your book, have at it. People who read e-books love them. Even writers of fiction and poetry can use links in their frontmatter and backmatter. Poets should use links in their contents pages, but contents (or a list of chapters) is not suggested for fiction—linked or unlinked. Kindle *does* support imbedded links (meaning you can hide the links behind the keywords that describe them).

- Use Word's Page Break feature between chapters, but do not make a blank page as you might for a print book. Word's Page Break feature is in its ribbon and it requires only a single click. Do not leave lots of space between chapters or sections. A single space is all that is needed. In fact, Barnes & Noble's e-reader, Nook, will not accept more than one blank line.
- You can use special formatting in your chapter headlines. Make them bold or larger than the body copy, but do not use fancy fonts (typefaces). Some readers (like Nook and Kindle) do not support the ornate ones. Arial, Verdana, and Times New Roman are safe bets. You can use italics, but I see no reason for the clutter. People will be reading on a screen, after all. Chapter subheads can also be given some attention with bold or larger typeface but, again, don't get fancy.
- If your book is nonfiction, mark the headings so you can make a table of contents with them—all automated and courtesy of Word. You should be able to find the heading formatter in the Word ribbon at the top of your screen. Alternatively, use Word's Help feature.
- Nonfiction e-books should have contents pages with live links so readers can skip easily to the sections or chapters they want to read. Use the **References** tab at the top of your Word screen to make a contents page automatically after you format each headline.
- You may want to use a more advanced formatting model than the one I am giving you

here if you use sidebars or lots of images in your nonfiction. (I give you a link to access a program for that below.) It is easier (but not as pretty) to set sidebar copy off with a row of tildes (~~~) and introduce it with a header that designates it as a sidebar. Close with a similar row of tildes. (Tildes *are* supported by the simple Kindle model.)

- You can also use all-caps for the first three or four words in every chapter or section. That helps cue the reader that he or she is beginning something new.
- The first page of your e-book is your title page or the image of your book cover if you prefer to do that page yourself. If not, Kindle provides an option that adds the image on the first page for you. In either case, the book cover image is on the first page and the title page ends up on the next page.
- If you do not have book cover art, Createspace.com provides a generic one for you—free. All their template choices have a similar look and limitations, but with some trial and error you can make one of them look quite presentable. To get an idea of how yours might look, see the ones my poetry coauthor Magdalena Ball and I use for our Celebration Series of chapbooks: howtodoitfrugally.com/poetry_books.htm.
- You may include the ISBN and disclaimers on your title page, but keep it simple.
- Here is a tip that no one seems to tell those of us who love our frontmatter—you know—our

acknowledgments, dedications, etc. Kindle's converter eliminates them if you leave them in the front of the book where you are accustomed to seeing them. Besides, Kindle readers can sample your book on Amazon, typically the first ten pages. If those ten pages are frontmatter filler, you might lose a sale. Your e-book must start with the cover image/title page with copyright info and the first chapter. Therefore, I cheat. I move selected pieces of my frontmatter to the end of my book. It is important to thank people, and is a shame not to put acknowledgements somewhere.

- It is acceptable to add information about your other e-books or forthcoming ones to the backmatter of your book. Why not? It is something I often suggest to my clients.

- Some authors even charge for a couple of sponsor ads in the back to offset the cost of publishing. Be sure to use live links to advertisers' sales pages. Read a short blog post I wrote on paid advertising in your books and a program offered by Amazon for Kindle Fire at bit.ly/BookSponsors.

- Be sure to proofread the whole book once it is set up as an e-book. You have made a lot of changes, right? And Kindle's conversion isn't perfect. We all know that changes beget typos.

- When you're satisfied, save your e-book text and format *with these special instructions* from Amazon: "Once you have inserted your page breaks and are confident with the layout of your book, save your Word file to your Documents folder or Desktop in **Web Page, Filtered (*HTM & *HTML)** (for PC) or **Web Page (.htm)** (for Mac) format. This format is required to build a successful eBook. "

- Now you're ready to sign in to Kindle (kdp.amazon.com/self-publishing/signin) or start an account. Upload your cover and Word file as instructed on their Web site. Don't neglect to sign up for all applicable sales benefits Amazon offers their loyal Select program members. That program requires an e-book exclusive on Kindle for six months and is a great marketing tool for an e-book launch. See the blog post I wrote just before Amazon's initial announcement on one of their newer benefits called Kindle Unlimited (http://bit.ly/KindleUnlimitedRoyalties).

- If you have advanced formatting needs or ideas (picture book anyone?) use this link for detailed instructions and a free program download that will make it happen for you: http://bit.ly/Detailsf4PubbingImages.

- Here is a link for updated information on formatting from Kindle using your Word program: bit.ly/FormattingKind.

APPENDIX SEVEN
OTHER FRUGAL RESOURCES FOR WRITERS

I remember how hard it was to find a publisher, participate in the galley process, and market my first book. This in spite of many years as a professional journalist, publicist, and marketer. That is why I provide so many helps for writers, many of them free. I hope what I do will keep other writers from falling into the same potholes I did and give them the resources they need to build writing careers.

- The Resources for Writers segment of my HowToDoItFrugally Web site includes several helpful lists rarely seen on other writers' portals including lists of Masters of Fine Arts programs for writers, media release distributors, digital presses, and accessible and legitimate contests. (howtodoitfrugally.com)

- *SharingwithWriters* newsletter is my free curated collection of news, opinions, and how-tos on building a writing career. It is also a community where you share your ideas and learn from others'. Everything from a poetry corner to promotion to craft to editing tips—all frugally. Subscribe at howtodoitfrugally.com.

- *SharingwithWriters* blog covers book promotion, publishing, and the art of writing and was named to Writer's Digest 101 Best Websites. (Writer's Digest's style choice is *Websites*.) It even has its own search engine so you can find posts on the topics important to you. (sharingwithwriters.blogspot.com)

- *The Frugal, Smart, and Tuned-In Editor* is where I post more on wordiness and pet peeves. I encourage guest posts, including yours. Read posts on things like how I flunked *Time* magazine's initialism test and more at TheFrugalEditor.blogspot.com.

- *The New Book Review* is a blog where authors, reviewers and readers recycle their favorite reviews absolutely free. Follow the submission guidelines on the left of the blog homepage as carefully as if you were entering a literary contest. (TheNewBookReview.blogspot.com)

ABOUT THE AUTHOR

Carolyn Howard-Johnson's several careers prepared her for promoting her own books and those of others and for editing many genres from nonfiction to poetry. She was the youngest person ever hired as a staff writer for *The Salt Lake Tribune*—"A Great Pulitzer Prize Winning Newspaper"—where she wrote features for the society page and a column under the name of Debra Paige. That gave her insight into the needs of editors, the very people authors must work with to get free ink and the ones likely to spot unprofessional editing when they see it. Being familiar with the way news is handled helps her see how the topics and premises of different books fit into different news cycles.

Later in New York, she was an editorial assistant at *Good Housekeeping Magazine* and handled accounts for fashion publicist Eleanor Lambert who instituted the first Ten Best Dressed List. She wrote media releases (then called press releases) for celebrity designers of the day including Pauline Trigere, Rudy Gernreich, and Christian Dior and directed photo shoots for Lambert's clients.

She also worked as columnist, reviewer, and staff writer for the *Pasadena Star-News, Home Décor Buyer*, the *Glendale News-Press* (an affiliate of the *LA Times*), Myshelf.com, and others.

She learned marketing skills both in college (University of Utah, and University of Southern

California) and as founder and operator of a chain of retail stores. That molded her understanding of how authors might best collaborate with retailers to affect both of their bottom lines.

Carolyn's experience in journalism and as a poet and author of fiction and nonfiction helped the multi award-winning author understand how different genres can be marketed more effectively. She was an instructor for UCLA Extension's renowned Writers' Program for nearly a decade and earned an instructor's certificate from that school. She studied writing at Cambridge University, United Kingdom; Herzen University in St. Petersburg, Russia; and Charles University in Prague.

She turned her knowledge toward helping other writers with her HowToDoItFrugally series of books for writers. Her marketing campaign for the first edition of this book won the Next Generation Indie Best Book Award, Reader Views Award, and USA Book News Award. She also has a multi award-winning series of HowToDoItFrugally books for retailers.

Carolyn was honored as Woman of the Year in Arts and Entertainment by California Legislature members Carol Liu, Dario Frommer, and Jack Scott. She received her community's Character and Ethics award for promoting tolerance with her writing and the Diamond Award in Arts and Culture. She was named to *Pasadena Weekly's* list of fourteen women of "San Gabriel Valley women who make life happen" and Delta Gamma, a national fraternity of women, honored her with their Oxford Award.

Carolyn is an actor who has appeared in ads including Apple, Lenscrafters, Time-Life CDs, Disney

Cruises (Japan), and Blue Shield and has presented at writers' conferences and tradeshows across the US.

Carolyn admits to reading even for pleasure with a pencil in hand and to sometimes editing when she is in far-flung places like Tibet.

Author Photo by Uriah Carr

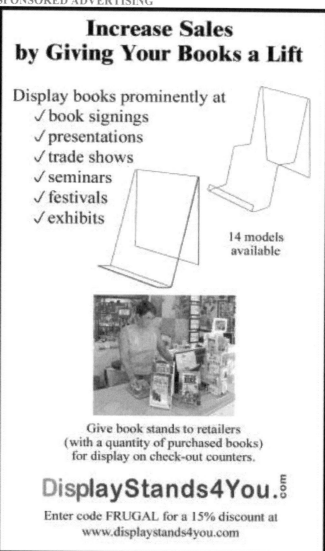
Advertise in future HowToDoItFrugally books. Contact Carolyn at
HoJoNews@aol.com.

Index

Numerals

60 Minutes (TV series), 186

A

A Word Please (newspaper column), 176
ABCs of POD, The (book), 241
Abkemeier, Laurie (agent), 65, 245
accent. See custom dictionaries, vocabulary.
acquisition editors. See editors.
Adams, Jenoyne (agent), 68, 245
address labels, 227-28
adjectives, 49, 62, 78, 115, 121 182, 188
    adjective predicate, 179
    adjectives, double, 174
advance readers, 195-200. Also see peer reviews.
adverbs, 38, 78, 107-16, 176, 179-81, 237, 280
    adverbs, placement, 129
advertising, 213, 260
agents, xvi, xxi, xxiv, xxvi, 36, 47, 49, 116, 200, 225, 231, 245-46
    agents' guidelines, 61, 69
    agents' pet peeves, 61-70
Agnew, Spiro, 182
Agni (periodical), 191
agreement, grammatical, 55-57
AKA Literary, 68, 246
all right vs. alright, 179
all-caps, 145, 259
alliteration, 34, 123
already vs. all ready, 181

American Heritage Book of English Usage, The (reference), 189
American Society of Indexers, 215
American Typewriter (font), v
Amir, Nina (author), 240
ampersands, 155-56
Amtrak, 158
anecdotes, 131, 178
Angela's Ashes (book), 132
Angell, Roger (author), 34, 113, 240
apologies, in queries, 51
apostrophes, xxvi, 60, 102, 156-63
Apple (computer), 266
Appleton, Victor (author), 108
Arial (font), 37, 100, 258
as well as, 112. Also see redundancy.
ASIN, 180
Associated Press (AP), 184, 203, 221, 234, 238
Associated Press Stylebook (reference), 238
Association of Mormon Letters, 153
assonance, 34
at the end of the day, wordiness, 186
attachments, e-mail, 230
Atwood, Megan C. (agent), 61, 69
AutoCorrect functions, 98-103
autosignature, e-mail, 42, 235
awesome, overuse, 49, 78
awhile vs. a while, 180

B

backmatter, 209, 212-15, 220, 257-60
Bailee, Dehanna (author), 241
Ball, Magdalena (author), xvi, 259
Band-Aid, 87
because of, wordiness, 187
Bent, Jenny (agent), 64, 245
bestsellers, 64
Bete, Tim (author), xvi
between, misuse, 56-57, 183
big gloom, 202
Blue Shield, 267
blurbs, 153, 179, 214
book bigotry, avoiding, 221
book industry, 96
book proposals, xxi, 68-69, 182, 242, 286
Book Proposals That Sell (book), 242
boots on the ground (cliché), 186
Bowerman, Peter (author), xvi, 242
branding, xx, xxvi, 41-42, 52, 235
Brown Literary Agency, 64, 245
Brown, Roberta (agent), 64, 245
Bryson, Bill (author), 238
Bryson's Dictionary of Troublesome Words (reference), 238
Bugs Bunny, 255
busing vs. bussing, 94
buy vs. purchase, 50

C

capitalization, 54, 95. Also see all-caps.
Carlson, Roger, computer help, 237
Carroll, Lewis (author), 164
Cartwright, Gene (author), iv, xvi
Casagrande, June (author), 126, 172-73, 183, 239
Charles University, 266
checklist, editing, 235-36
Chiarella, Tom (author), 132, 153, 240
Chicago Manual of Style, The (reference), 34, 51-52, 93, 182, 185, 215, 222, 238-39
citations, academic, 155
acknowledgments, xv-xvii, 199, 259
Clark, Roy Peter (author), 109
clauses
    clause punctuation, 197
    clauses causing dangling participles, 118-21
    clause introducers, 189-92
clichés, xxi, 67, 114-15, 177, 185-86
Cliff Notes (booklets), 66
Clinton, Bill (quote), 98
Coca Cola (branding), 41, 253
cohabitate vs. cohabit, 181
collective terms, 56
colloquialisms, 149, 151
Complete Guide to Self-Publishing, The (book), 241
Complete Manual of Typography, The (book), 242
Complete Rhyming Dictionary, The (reference), 34, 286

Complete Writer's Journal, The (book), 55
computer
    computer confusion, 35-36
    computer edits, 71-98, 266
    computer shortcuts, 98-103
Concordance, 79, 81, 237
conferences, writers', 70, 120, 153, 203
conjunctions, 184
    conjunctions (beginning sentences), 60, 87
    conjunctions, titles, 54
contents page, 214, 254, 257-58
contests, 37, 70, 223, 243, 249, 263
copyright, 35, 99, 101, 259-60
copywriting, for pharmaceutical ads, 127
corrections, tracking, 46, 75, 78, 148, 154, 196, 210
cover letters. See query letters.
Crawford, JayCe (author), xxi, 97, 111
Createspace, 259
credentials, xx, 30, 51, 63, 67, 203, 206
Cron, Lisa (author), xxiii, 146, 240
custom dictionaries. See dictionaries.
Cup of Comfort, A (book series), 111

D

dangling participles. See participles.
dashes, 164-65, 174, 185-86, 197
    dashes in dialogue, 138, 172
    dashes, em, 185

dashes, en, 185
dedications in e-books, 259
Deen, Paula (TV personality), 188
DeFiore and Company, 65, 245
degeneration, grammar, 178-79
denouement, 202
Describer's Dictionary, The (book), 34, 240
design, book interiors, 219-20
DeSimone, Chaz (cover artist), iv, v, xvi, 156, 212, 220
desktops, 33-37
dialect, 34, 87, 89, 91, 111, 162. Also see dialogue.
dialectical marks, 103
dialogue, 31, 78, 108, 110, 131, 150, 153, 178, 181, 184, 240
    dialogue, italics, 146-48
    dialogue, direct questions, 154
    dialogue, internal. See italics.
    dialogue, natural pauses. See ellipses.
    dialogue, passive construction, 126-27
    dialogue, protocol, 149
    dialogue punctuation, 132, 136-39, 153, 216
    dialogue tags, 31, 46, 108, 132, 139
dictionaries, 167, 173
    dictionaries, custom, 87-91, 93, 112, 241
    dictionaries, vocabulary, 34, 88
Dior, Christian (designer), 265
disclaimers, 197, 259
Disney Cruises, Japan, 266

dissertations, 83, 184, 239, 276
due to, wordiness, 187

E

Eagan, Scott (agent), 62, 245
Eats, Shoots & Leaves (book),
    169, 176, 238
e-book vs. ebook, 94-95
editing. See this book's
    Contents.
    editing, definitions, 29
    editing, dialogue, 135-45
    editing, by hand, 163
    editing, final galley, 210-36
editors, v, x, xix, xxiii-xv,
    49, 73, 190, 200, 204-05,
    210, 219, 238, 246
    editors, cost, 10, 202-03,
    206-207
effete, misuse, 182
Ekus-Saffer, Lisa (agent), 62,
    245, 276
Eleanor Lambert Publicity, 263
Elements of Style (reference),
    34, 113, 240
ellipses, 152-54, 216. Also see
    dialogue.
e-mail, 42, 143, 152, 229-36
    e-mail signatures, 42, 231
    e-mail submission services,
    67
e-mail vs. email, 94
emphasis, 148-49. Also see
    italics.
endorsements. See blurbs.
Endust (brand name), 83
English, xix, 103, 111, 125,
    129, 159, 162, 166, 177, 199
    Also see dialogue, idioms.
    English teachers, 31

English, Elaine P. (agent), 63,
    245
enormity vs. enormous, 182
entitled vs. titled, 24, 50, 182
errors, cut-and-paste, 57, 59-60
et cetera, &c. vs. ampersand,
    abbreviation, 155
ethnicity, 276
Excel (computer program), 96
exclamation points, 67, 90, 138,
    152, 229
expletives, 125
exposition, 135
extra spaces, 82-83, 235

F

Far From the Madding Gerund
    (book), 238
Far from Heaven (film), 253
Farrar, Straus and Giroux, xv,
    121
Faulkner, Joyce (author), xv,
    64
FedEx, 226
Felici, Jim (author), 242
Ferris Buehler's Day Off
    (film), 127
fiction writers, 34, 74, 153,
    178, 240, 247
Find Function, 78-80, 95, 107,
    109, 111, 117, 119, 121-23,
    133, 139, 148, 150, 154,
    161, 163, 207
findability, 98
Finishing Line Press, 165
Firebrand Literary Agency, 61
first person, 147, 252
Folio Literary Management, 64
font, v, 37, 47, 63, 77, 100, 145,
    212, 247, 256, 258. Also see
    typefaces.

foreword vs. preface, 220-21
formatter, 82, 85, 145, 154,
    211-16, 236, 258
formatting symbols, 82, 101,
    210
Fresh Books Literary Agency,
    62, 246
frontmatter, 213-14, 220, 257,
    259-60
Frugal and Focused Tweeting
    for Retailers (book), viii
Frugal Book Promoter, The
    (book), viii, xx, 41-42, 52,
    66, 68, 98, 219, 235, 242
Frugal Editor, The (book), xxii,
    xxvi, 95
Full Circle Literary LLC, 62,
    245
future perfect, past perfect. See
    tenses.

G

galley, xxvi, 29, 46, 209-25,
    236
    galley edits, 209-12
Garner, Bryan A. (author), 93,
    238
Garner's Modern American
    Usage (reference), 93, 238
General Motors, 41
George, Elizabeth (author), 148
Gernreich, Rudy (designer), 265
gerunds, 117-22, 238, 276
Ghahremani, Lily (agent), 62,
    245
Glendale News-Press, 265
Glimmer Train (periodical), 249
Gogolewski, Kathe (author),
    xvi, 47, 211
Good Housekeeping Magazine,
    248, 265

Gorham Printing, 222
grade level, writing for, 92
Grambs, David (author), 34,
    240
grammar errors, xx-xxiv, 30, 86
Grammar Snobs Are Big
    Meanies (book), 239
grammatical expertise,
    technique. See dialogue.
Great First Impression Book
    Proposal, The (booklet), 242
Great Little Last-Minute
    Editing Tips for Writers
    (booklet), viii, 185
Greyhaus Literary Agency, 62,
    245
guess what, misuse, 183
guidelines
    guidelines for contests
        submissions, 37, 70
    guidelines for e-books, 213-
        14
    guidelines for agent
        submissions, 61, 69, 228,
        236, 262

H

Hancock Murray, Tamela
    (agent), 65, 246
hardcopy, 33, 36, 46, 49, 73,
    150, 225, 227, 235
HarperCollins, 179
Harry Potter, 176
Hartline Literary Agency, 65
hashtags, 38
header/footer function, 36-37,
    67, 257
headings, subheadings, 212-
    216, 257-58
Herzen University, 70, 266

Home Décor Buyer (periodical), 265
hook (structure), 66, 138
Hosseini, Khaled (author), 88
How to Blog a Book (book), 240
How to Publish and Promote Your Book Now (book), 242
How to Write a Book Proposal (book), 242
Humera (pharmaceutical), 129
humor, 116, 119, 149, 254
hyphens, 95, 100-02, 168-75, 188

I

I think, I believe, usage, 50
idioms, English, 115, 237
Iglesias, Karl (author), 240
imagery, 114-15. Also see metaphors, similes, symbols.
in order to, wordiness, 187
indents, uses, 68, 147, 196, 257
Independent Book Publishers Association (IBPA), 219
InDesign (computer program), 216
indexes, xxvi, 102, 197, 215, 237
indexes, e-books, 226
infinitives, split, 112-13
ing, ed, en. See participles.
intent. See voice, passive.
iPhone, 158
IRC (International Reply Coupon), 228
irony, 149-50. Also see italics.
ISBN, 180, 259
italics, 134, 144, 146-150, 255. Also see dialogue.

J

jargon, 34, 81, 87-88, 91, 111
Jet Literary Agency, 63, 246
Johnson, Kristin (author), xvi 254
Jose, Virgil (editor), 238
journalism, 240, 266

K

kerning, typesetting, 83
Kessler, Lauren (author), 240
keywords, 54, 81, 98, 197, 237
Kindle Fire, 260
Kindle, formatting, 242, 256-61
King, Stephen (author), 139
Kirshbaum, Larry (agent), 68
Kite Runner, The (book), 88
Kleinman, Jeff (agent), 64
Krygier, Leora (author), xvi, 29, 74, 132-33
KT Public Relations & Literary Services, 63, 246

L

LA Times. See Los Angeles Times.
Lamb, Wally (author), 179
Lamisil (pharmaceutical), xxiv
language, 88, 94-96, 103, 111, 114, 120, 126-27, 129, 144, 154, 159-62, 166, 176 - 77, 179-80, 188, 239
language, foreign symbols, 103
Lapsing Into a Coma: A Curmudgeon's Guide to the Many Things That Can Go Wrong (book), 237

Larsen, Michael (agent), 63, 70,
   242, 245
Latinate words, 50
Lenscrafter, 265
letterhead, 41-42, 228
Levine/Greenberg Literary
   Agency, Inc., 63, 68, 246
line editing, definition, 30
links, 54, 188, 256-59
Lisa Ekus Public Relations Co.
   LLC, 62, 245
lists, 223, 226, 261
   list, adverbs, 109-113
   list, agents, 61-70, 229. Also
     see Appendix Three.
   list, using advance readers.
     See advance readers.
   list, computer shortcuts, 101-
     02
   list, desktop essentials, 33-35
   list, editing checklist, 235-36
   list, editors, 234
   list, errors, 179-85. Also see
     wordiness, clichés,
     politically correct.
   list, hiring editors, 198, 203-
     06
   list, writers' resources, 108,
     223, 236-40, 263
   list, verbs helping, 123
   list, prepositions, 57
literally vs. figuratively, 183
literally vs. virtually, 49
literary agents. See agents, list
   in Appendix Three.
live vs. reside, 50
LJK Literary, 68
loglines, 66-67
logos, 42, 220
Look Inside feature (Amazon),
   132
Los Angeles Times, 94, 188,

26
Luminosity.com (Web site),
   101

M

Mac, computer, 36, 260
Maguire, Kristie Leigh (author),
   xv
Maines, Leah (editor), 165
Making the Perfect Pitch
   (book), 241
manual edits, 45-46, 55, 59, 75,
   78, 80, 83-85, 145-48, 150,
   163, 169, 195-200, 235
Manual for Writers of Research
   Papers, Theses, and
   Dissertations, 239
manuscript boxes, 227
manuscripts, xxi-xxiv, 29,
   31, 35-38, 45-47, 62-75, 82,
   93, 112, 145, 148, 195-97,
   200-03, 209, 211, 256
   manuscript, mailing, 226-36,
     247
MatchBook feature (Amazon),
   69
McCourt, Frank (author), 132
McDonald, Duncan (author),
   240
McMurrin, Trudy (editor), vii,
   xvi
McNichol, Barbara (editor),
   xxiii, 237
media disseminators, 223
media kits, xxii, 182, 201, 232,
   247-48
media release, v, 38, 181-82,
   201, 223, 263
media release vs. press release,
   42
memoirs, 68, 132, 138, 182

metal vs. medal, 196
metaphors, 114-16, 186, 199
Michael Larsen–Elizabeth
    Pomada Literary Agents, 63,
    245
Missouri Review, The
    (periodical), 191
Moore, Julianne (actor), 253
Morelli, Linda (author), 198
Mortal Syntax: 101 Language
    Choices That Will Get You
    Clobbered (book), 239
Mother Goose's Nursery
    Rhymes (book), 136
motivation, character, 202
moving forward, wordiness,
    186
myriad, misuse, 182

N

narrative, 123, 135, 178
Nelson Literary Agency LLC,
    66, 246
Nelson, Kristin (agent), 65-66,
    246
New Book Review, The (blog),
    264
New Fowler's Modern English
    Usage, The (reference), 239
New York Times, The, 51, 66,
    74, 94, 191
New Yorker, The (periodical),
    xix, 154, 191
news, current, 42
Newton, Diane (author), 209
Next Generation Indie Best
    Book Award, 266
Nook, 258
noun, false, 126. Also see
    passive voice.
novel vs. fictional novel, 50, 63

numbers vs. numerals, 100,
    184-85

O

obfuscation, 126. Also see
    passive voice.
omissions, 161-62. See
    apostrophes.
Onedrive (Microsoft cloud), 36
op-ed, 100
organizing desktops. See
    desktops.
Oriental Press (Publisher), xvi,
    253-54
orientated vs. oriented, 181
orphans, xxiv, 212-13. Also see
    widows.
Oxford English Dictionary, 167

P

pacing, 90. Also see passive
    voice.
Page Break feature, 212, 257-
    58, 260
page counts, 92
page headers, 36-37, 68, 145,
    153, 257, 259
page layout (manuscripts),
    36
page numbers, 36, 214, 221,
    257
page numbers, e-books, 226
PageMaker, 216
page-turning effect. See pacing,
    dialogue.
Panettieri, Gina (agent), 67, 246
paperclips, 37
paperclips vs. staples, 227
paragraph indentations, 67.
    Also see indents.

paragraph marks (¶), 82
participles, xix, 117-18, 121-22
    participles, dangling, 118-22
Pasadena Star-News, 265
Pasadena Weekly, 266
passive voice, 39, 78, 125-29, 135, 157, 169, 187, 237. Also see tenses.
Penguin (publisher), 239
peer reviews, 197-98. Also see advance readers.
people vs. persons, 181
Perrin and Smith Handbook of Current English (book), 230
Perry, Yvonne (editor), 238
photograph, author, iv, 216, 227
picture books, 261
platforms, 68, 94
PLLC Literary, 63, 245
plot points, 66-67, 202
plurals, 26, 55-56, 156-62, 181
poetry, 37, 53, 153, 165-66, 227, 243, 263
point of view (POV), 134, 147, 156, 178. Also see italics.
politically correct, 185-89
Pomada, Elizabeth (agent), 63, 245
possessives, 156-61, 163
Post-it notes, 46, 196
Poynter, Dan (author), 95
prefixes, 166-67, 170-73
Premarin (pharmaceutical), 129
prepositions, 121-22, 128, 160, 180, 183, 237
    prepositions, agreement, 54-57
preventative vs. preventive, 181
printouts, 45, 195
producers, xxi, 191, 232
pronoun/antecedent errors, 55-56
proofreading. See editors.
    proofreading, definitions, 29-30
    proofreading marks, 210
publishers, formatting, 211-21
publishing
    publishing info, free, 222
    publishing process, 30, 36, 49, 68-70, 111, 154, 170, 176, 184, 201, 204, 209-16, 219-20, 227, 231, 240, 245-47
    publishing, self, 85, 143, 146, 154, 170, 197, 209, 221-23, 241-42
Pulitzer (prize), 211
Pullum, Geoffrey K. (author), 238
punctuation, 30, 90, 136-39, 164, 174, 176, 238
    punctuation, British, 136, 167, 176
    punctuation, dialogue, 136-38, 152, 216
Purdue University, 127, 156-58

Q

query letters, xxi-xxii, 41, 49-50, 64-70, 98, 120-23, 181-82, 228-29, 247-48
query templates, 64, 250-54
Quinn, Robin (editor), 189, 238
quotation marks, 76, 121, 132-35, 137-38, 146
    quotation marks, curly, 60, 96, 100, 138
quotations, 131, 153, 240
quote vs. quotation, 179-80

R

race, politically correct, 188
reach out, misuse, 187
Readability Statistics, 79,
    90-93, 128
Reader Views Award, 266
Reader's Digest (periodical),
    114
readers vs. experts, 198
reading groups, 215
Red Engine Press, xv, 55
Redford, Robert (director), 251-
    52
redundancy, 78, 107, 112, 115,
    139, 152, 180, 214
Reel, David (author), 255
reference books, 33-35, 39,
    185, 226-27, 237. Also see
    recommended books in
    Appendix Seven.
references, referrals, 202, 205-
    06, 222
regardless vs. irregardless, 180
repetitive words, 78, 111, 133
Replace All tool, 75-78, 82-84
requested material, 228
resources for writers. See
    Appendix Seven.
Retailer's Guide to Frugal In-
    Store Promotions, A (book),
    viii
revision, xxiii, 29-31, 45-46, 66,
    132-33, 135, 148, 198
revision (definition), 29
rhyme, 34, 123, 136. Also see
    poetry.
Rich, Dr. Bob (author), xvi, 36,
    73, 80, 147, 238
Ridgway, Peggi (author), xvi
Ross, Marilyn (author), xvi, 242
Rostan, Stephanie Kip (agent),
    63, 241
rules, grammar, 31, 34, 113-14,
    117, 136, 158
rules, Web, 164
rules vs. style choice, 206,
    239
Rutgers University, 127
Ryan, Meg (actor), 50

S

sales benefits, Amazon, 261
Salt Lake Tribune, The, 248
Sands, Katherine (author), 241
sans serif typeface, 37
sarcasm, 149-50
SASE (Self-Addressed Stamped
    Envelope), 227
scams, avoiding, 202-05
scientific terms, 34, 91, 241
Secrets II (book), 209
Select program, Amazon, 261
Selfin, Peter (editor), xix-xx
serial commas, 156, 184
settings, writing craft, xxii
SharingwithWriters blog, 263-
    64, 271
SharingwithWriters newsletter,
    79, 180, 264, 271
should, using, 125
sidebars, 39, 47, 53-54, 65, 77,
    79-81, 84-85, 89-91, 93,
    97, 99-103, 109-10, 113,
    128, 137-38, 151, 154, 159-
    60, 161-63, 168, 170-73,
    175, 203-05, 221
    sidebar, formatting, 258-59
    sidebar, placement, 213
sign makers, v, 156-57
signatures, e-mail, 42, 231, 235

Silverman, Francine (author) 241
similes. See imagery, metaphors, symbols.
Simon & Schuster, 51
Simpsons, The, 184
since vs. because, 182-83
sinkage, formatting, 211
Skydrive. See Onedrive.
slang, 149, 151, 182
Small Publishers of North America (SPAN), 114
Smithsonian, The (periodical), 191
snuck vs. sneaked, 184
South Fork Pictures, 252
space requirements, 92
spacebar, 82-85, 120, 154. Also see computer, formatting.
spam, 230
speech patterns, 78, 110, 118, 133. Also see dialogue.
Spelling and Grammar Checker, 35, 38-39, 59, 85-87, 89-90, 93, 167-68, 171, 173
Spiekermann, Erik (author), 242
spitting image vs. spit and image, 181
sponsorships, 260, Also see advertising.
Starbucks, 97
stationery, 42, 228, 235
Steve Laube Agency, 246
Stop Stealing Sheep and Find Out How Type Works (book), 242
structure, xxi, xxiii, 30-31, 46, 66, 92, 119, 139, 185, 192, 206, 222
Strunk and White. See Elements of Style and Strunk.
Strunk Jr, William (author), 34-

35, 113-14, 121-22, 240
Strunk, White, and Angell (authors). See Elements of Style.
study guides, 215
style choices, 34-35, 74-75, 87-88, 94, 103, 114, 122, 132, 147, 155-56, 164, 206, 239, 263
stylebooks, 34, 93-95, 136, 159, 169, 172-73, 188, 238
subject lines, 42, 229-30
submissions, exclusive, 69-70
submitting manuscripts, 36, 55, 67-69, 200, 225-27, 236
subplots, 66
subtitles, 54, 98, 145, 196
suffixes, 166, 171
summaries, 66. Also see synopses.
Summer Literary Semesters, 70
Sun Signs for Writers (book), 242
Swisher (brand name), 41
Symbol function, 82, 101, 151, 180
symbols for editing, 210
synopses, 66, 203. Also see summaries.

T

taglines, 66, 108-09. Also see dialogue tags.
Talcott Notch Literary, 67, 246
Talk Radio Wants You (book), 241
tech terms, 34. Also see dictionaries.
Ten Speed Press (publisher), xxiii, 146

tenses, 66, 118, 122-23, 178,
186, 255. Also see verbs,
helper.
tension. See pacing, dialogue,
exposition.
thank yous, 231
the, in titles, 51-52
the fact that, wordiness, 187
the reason for, wordiness, 186
thesaurus, 34, 78
Thesaurus function, 108
thesis, academic, xxii, 83, 162,
184, 198, 239
third person, 146, 255
Thomas, Michel (linguist), 122
Tienstra, Kae (agent), 63, 246
Time-Life CDs, 266
titled vs. entitled, 50
titles, xxiv, 34-37, 51-52, 69,
95, 98-100, 117, 144-45,
182, 188, 196, 214, 251
title pages, 258-260
to lie and to lay, 177-178
to raise and to rise, 178
Toastmasters, 110
Tom Swifties, 108
too, also, as well as, in addition
to, 112. Also see
redundancy.
Tracings (chapbook), 165
Tracker (word processer
feature), 75-78, 199
transom (publishing term), 251
Trident Media Group, 64
Trigere, Pauline (designer), 265
Trupin-Pulli, Liz (agent), 63,
246
Truss, Lynne (author), 169,
176, 238
try and vs. try to, 184
Turabian, Kate (author), 239
Twelve Years a Slave (film),

189
typefaces, v, 37, 95, 103, 145,
258
typography, 148, 242
typos, x, xvi, xx, xxii, xxiv-xxv,
30, 46, 51, 198, 260

U

UCLA Extension Writers'
Program, xv, 149, 266
understood words, 191, 151
understood in dialogue, 132
University of Southern
California (USC), 265
United States Postal Service
(USPS), 227-28
University of Utah, 265
USA Book News Award, 266

V

Venis, Linda (educator), xv
verbs. Also see tenses, dialogue.
verbs, helper, 118-26, 178
verbs, strong, 66, 78, 107,
134
viruses, computer, 143, 230
vocabularies, 34, 91, 111
Also see dictionaries, custom
dictionaries.
vocabulary, regional, 88. Also
see dialect.
voice, xx-xxi, 78, 126-27, 129,
134, 139, 169, 254-55 Also
see tense, verbs, passive.

W

Wagner, Matt (agent), 62, 246
Walsh, Bill (author), 237

Walton-Porter, Bev, (author), 242
We Are Water (book), 179
Web site vs. Website, 51, 74, 94
Well-Fed Self-Publisher, The (book), 242
Whalin, Terry (author), 242
What Foreigners Need To Know About America From A To Z (book), xvi, 225, 253
When She Sleeps (book), 74
When Words Collide: A Media Writer's Guide to Grammar and Style (book), 240
White, E. B. (author), 34, 113, 121, 240
who vs. that, 216
widows, xiv, 212-213. Also see orphans.
Wikipedia, 155
Wired for Story (book), xxiii, 146, 240
Wolf, Terrie (agent), 68, 246
Wolfe, L. Diane (author), 242
Wolfson Literary, 279
Wolfson, Michelle (agent), 65, 246
Wood, Clement (author), 34
Word's tools, 73
    Word's dictionary, 79, 88, 93, 89-91. Also see dictionaries.
    Word's thesaurus. See thesaurus.
    Word's tracker. See tracker.
wordiness, xxi, 39, 49, 123, 177, 185-86, 264. Also see redundancy, adverbs.
wordtrippers, viii, 185
Writer's Digest (periodical), 116
Writer's Digest (publisher), 132, 153, 240, 242-43
Writer's Digest 101 Best Websites (resource), 263, 271
Writer's Market (reference), 243
Writers Guild of America, 155
Writing Dialogue (book), 132, 153, 240
Writing for Emotional Impact (book), 240

Y

y'know. 109-110. See adverbs, redundancy, wordiness.
young adult (YA), 92
Your Blog, Your Business (book), viii

Made in the USA
San Bernardino, CA
26 March 2019